D0810231

THE TIME OF MY LIFE

THE TIME OF MY LIFE

A RIGHTEOUS BROTHER'S MEMOIR

BILL MEDLEY

with Mike Marino

Da Capo Press
A Member of the Perseus Books Group

Designed by Jill Shaffer
Set in 12-point Warnock Pro by Eclipse Publishing Services

Cataloging-in-Publication data for this book is available from the Library of Congress.

ISBN: 978-0-306-82316-9
E-book ISBN: 978-0-306-82317-6

Published by Da Capo Press
A Member of the Perseus Books Group
www.dacapopress.com

Da Capo Press books are available at special discounts for bulk purchases in the U.S. by corporations, institutions, and other organizations. For more information, please contact the Special Markets Department at the Perseus Books Group, 2300 Chestnut Street, Suite 200, Philadelphia, PA 19103, or call (800) 810-4145, ext. 5000, or e-mail special.markets@perseusbooks.com.

10 9 8 7 6 5 4 3 2 1

Contents

Foreword

I still remember the first time I heard Bill Medley's deep, soulful baritone booming through my little Zenith 500 transistor radio.

It was the summer of 1964 and I was fifteen years old, checking out the girls with my friends on Jones Beach, Long Island.

"You've Lost That Lovin' Feelin'" was about to explode into the sonic boom heard around the world.

"You never close your eyes anymore when I kiss your lips" hit me—and every other guy who heard it—right in the gut.

His voice personified the sound of a man wounded by love. It was a righteous epiphany.

And it would forever herald the opening theme to the opera of our adolescence.

It still hits me in the gut every time I hear it—like the four-note entry motif of Beethoven's Fifth.

Bill Medley's voice resonates to this day—and his journey through life explains the depth and soul inherent in that voice.

–Billy Joel

Preface

I've had a life . . . and then some. Through some really great highs and some amazing lows my life has gone far deeper than I ever imagined it would. My ex-wife was brutally murdered; I lost my voice completely and was told I'd never sing again; I had hit records in four different decades, performed in dive bars and for the president of the United States.

When I do concerts I'm asked tons of questions. "How did the Righteous Brothers get their name? Did you and Bobby Hatfield get along? What was Phil Spector really like? Why did the Beatles and the Rolling Stones pick you guys to perform on their first American tours?"

So, I started doing a storytelling portion in my show. Now people come up to me afterwards and say, "Man, I love the show but in the second half, where you did that story-telling thing, that was unbelievably cool." I know if I had the chance to sit down with Ray Charles or Little Richard or any of those guys and ask them what they were thinking when they did this or that, I would love it. Hearing the song is great—but *why* you did it and how you *felt* when you did it is almost as important as the song itself, because you can hear the song at home.

Of course there are some things I'd like to clear up. All through our career, for some reason, people thought that Bobby and I disliked each other. That's not true, our relationship was very complicated, we were like brothers—and brothers don't always see eye to eye. Bobby and I were very different, as you'll discover in the pages that follow. We were really young when we became successful and it affected us both in very different ways.

I learned that success includes great responsibility—like it or not. A lot of artists have an "I don't give a shit" attitude, which I understand, but that's not me. When you have success people look at you with a magnifying glass and I've always felt something of an obligation, as corny as it sounds, to be a role model. I didn't sign up for that, but it's part of the gig. God knows, as you'll discover in this book, I haven't always hit the bull's-eye in that regard, but that's how I feel. Ever since we had our first big hits I knew every time I walked out of the house people were going to want to talk to me, get an autograph, or take a picture. For me, it's either screw my head onto that or stay home, period.

I'm actually honored that people still care about the stories and the music. Writing this book has shown me how blessed I've been in many ways. People often comment about how the Righteous Brothers changed the face of American music and helped usher in the "blue-eyed soul" era, which I take as a wonderful compliment. Ironically, there was nothing about the Righteous Brothers that should have worked—but it did. Let me tell you how and why in this book. I hope along the way I'll make you smile, maybe cry a bit, and at the end of the story feel like you know who Bill Medley is.

My last hit record was "(I've Had) the Time of My Life." I chose that for the title of this book because I really have had an incredible life filled with a lot of joy, deep friendships, and some big-time, lesson-learning pain. Thankfully, it's not over, I still learn every day. One lesson I've learned is to appreciate it when people take time to be interested in you. Thanks for investing a piece of your life in learning about mine.

1 | Orange County Graffiti

If you've ever watched the movie *American Graffiti* or seen the TV show *Happy Days* you have a good picture of what it was like growing up in Orange County, California, in the 1950s and early 1960s.

Our hangout was Fiduccia's Gas Station. Frank Fiduccia's sons were part of our crowd and their dad let us use his business for our headquarters. Why he let us hang around there I'll never know—we must have driven away customers. This was long before I met Bobby Hatfield, but even then we couldn't have been more different. He was the button-down president of his high-school class and I was the Levi's and T-shirt, greaser, motorcycle racing guy who absolutely hated school.

Boyhood friend Johnny Mohler Bill *was* Fonzie.
The duck-tail haircut, the leather jacket, everything.
He didn't do well in school except for choir, he loved
that. In those days when you started going out with
a girl you gave her your jacket to wear, instead of a
ring. Bill had at least three different jackets for three

1

different girls. They liked him so much because he was a real sweetheart, just a wonderful person and he hasn't changed a bit. The fame and fortune never changed him. Both Bill and my brother hated school so much they quit (or got kicked out depending on who tells the story) and both of them were millionaires before I even graduated.

I think a little bit of my Texas roots contributed to my boyhood rebellion and my feeling "different" from many of the other Orange County kids. My grandpa W.T. Medley, whom I'm named after, was born and raised in Texas. He had a cattle ranch in Van Horn, Texas, just west of El Paso. Eventually he lost it, came out West and acted in cowboy movies. My family wasn't great about keeping records so I don't know a lot about him, but I know he did well enough in the movies to return to Texas and buy his ranch back.

He was a real cowboy; he could ride, rope, and shoot. By all accounts he was a genuine Christian man nicknamed "the sweet man"—but he was not a guy to cross. There's a picture of him riding into town dragging the dead body of a horse thief he'd caught. Frontier justice. He died at age ninety-six walking to church.

It was at Grandpa's church that my dad Arnol met my mom Irma. Dad moved back to Texas, mom followed him there and they were married. In the late 1930s mom convinced dad to move back to California where they had a band, The Rhythm Hounds—she played piano and sang, and he played sax. Mom was also a hairdresser, which would later open the door for my brief and comical career in that field—details to follow.

Soon my sister Barbara and brother Leon came along, and I think my parents were mentally done with having kids. I was "the surprise" of 1940. Over the years I learned that I was not a happy surprise for my dad. I represented unwanted extra responsibility. I was a frustration for him and it showed all through my young years.

My brother and sister were angels, they really were. They never got in trouble, they never got spanked, and rightfully so—they never did anything wrong. My dad and I just collided. That's why, even today, I don't like to eat dinner, because every night at dinner my dad and I would get into it and he'd drag me away to spank me with a belt. He was a Texas guy and that's what they did. I was very defiant and I would fight him, I wouldn't let it go down easily. We would literally get in fistfights. If I had just taken a few whacks on the behind it would have been over, but I was a rebel and I fought back as hard as I could. One time in junior high, when I was taking a shower after PE class, one of the coaches asked me, "What's wrong with your back?" I had welts all over my back from my dad's beatings. I'm sure most teachers today would have told someone and my dad would have been in big trouble.

Bill's sister Barbara   Actually, our mom would get Bill into trouble with dad. It was one of those "wait until your father gets home" things, and then dad would have to discipline him. That always bothered me, the poor kid never got to sit at the dinner table through a whole meal. Mother would come up with something and dad would get irritated and poor Bill would get in trouble; it was sad. He wasn't really bad; he'd just do little things and all of a sudden dad was taking him away to spank him. It not only interrupted Bill's dinner, it interrupted Leon's and mine too. The funny

thing is, my dad thought the world of Bill; for the
most part he was a very good dad. But, the dinner
table was very hard on all of us.

In grammar school I developed these nervous head and stomach twitches. My aunt had similar twitches, and my mom always blamed my dad for bringing them out in me. They made me very self-conscious and embarrassed.

Maybe I'm just protecting my dad, but I never blamed him for the twitches. I still loved him, and as adults our relationship was much better. Once I was out of the house and successful as a Righteous Brother I think the pressure was off for him. He was a sheriff in charge of police communications. When he retired I flew in from Lake Tahoe for his retirement party. Some of the girls who worked with him took me aside to tell me how wonderful my dad was.

"He was so funny, always in a good mood. The sweetest, most gentle man we ever worked with."

I said, "Point him out to me."

That's when I learned that the dad who felt all this pressure at home, the dad who made both me and my mom nervous wrecks; the dad who only told me he loved me once and never hugged—that wasn't the man the world knew. In his later years I said "screw it" and started hugging him anyway. I know he wasn't comfortable with it, but he got used to it.

Still, the drama at home and my struggle with the nervous twitches made me an angry young man. I learned that the best way to keep people from making fun of me was to hit them. I fought a lot. I wasn't a big guy in those days; I was 5'3" until I was fifteen, and sang first tenor. Then I grew seven inches in one year and became a baritone, which made things a little easier.

Even though I had great friends, I became withdrawn and developed social anxiety, which I've struggled with my whole life. I think I used my rebel image and behavior as a defense. The leather jacket, greased-back hair, tough-guy crowd, the motorcycles—all just part of the Bill Medley protective mask.

Finally, the school sent me to a "shrink" and he told my mom, "This is a very lonely boy."

"What are you talking about, he has tons of friends," she said.

He repeated, "He's a very lonely boy."

Mom didn't get it, but I did. I was a very lonely, sad kid. I felt abandoned, my mom was always sick and my dad wasn't there for me emotionally. I still fight feelings of loneliness to this day. When I'm on the road I'm always on the phone, I don't like being alone.

The happier ending to the story is that through the years I felt I finally earned my dad's love, approval, and respect. I was able to take it in and that was healing in many ways. Getting to know the "other" Arnol Medley helped me understand who he really was, good and bad, as well as understand a little more about who I am.

The more I understood about who I really was, the less interested I was in school. I just hated it, except for choir class. My choir teacher was Jack Coleman. He turned out to be one of the most important men in my life. Not only did he encourage my musical ambitions, Jack literally saved my career and probably my life— much more about that later.

The second I turned sixteen I dropped out of school. "OK," I thought, "what am I going to do with my life?" I could sing like Little Richard, but what's a white kid from Orange County going to do with that? Because my mom was a hairdresser I thought I'd try hairdressing school. I enrolled at the Bartmore Beauty College on

Broadway Street in Santa Ana. The problem was I was still a greaser, and I was always cutting up and never studied.

Bartmore was a training school and little old ladies would come in to get their hair done because it was free. My first patron was a little old lady who had blue hair with pin curls. It looked like a little blue afro. I took the sweet lady to the sink and started shampooing her hair. Suddenly I looked down and her hair was gone. I picked up her head to see if it was in the sink and there was nothing, it scared the crap out of me. Great. My first client and I made them bald. I went to my teacher, Mrs. Woo, and said, "Her hair's gone!"

She shrieked, "What!" and ran over to the sink only to come back laughing hysterically. Because the lady's skin was so white, when I shampooed the blue out of her thin hair it blended into her white skin and you couldn't see it.

I flunked my state board exam, failing hair coloring and manicuring. I wouldn't learn manicures because you had to practice them near Bartmore's front window and I didn't want the kids walking home from school to see me doing a manicure. When I went to take the exam I copied everything the lady sitting next to me did. She must have failed manicuring too! Bartmore Beauty College was a great learning experience, but now I thank God I failed.

My Bartmore failure led me to my first (and thankfully only) giant musical failure. My friend Johnny Mohler said, "I know you can sing and I'm going to take you up to the Al Jarvis Talent Show." Al Jarvis was a popular Los Angeles radio and TV personality, sometimes called America's first radio "DJ." We went to the Paramount Theater in Los Angeles and there was this huge line to get in, and they only took about thirty people to perform. Mohler walked up and down the line saying, "Wait until you hear my friend sing, he can sing like Elvis, and he can sing anything!"

So, we finally go in and Al Jarvis asked, "Do you want any accompaniment?" I shook my head no. "OK, go ahead." You have to remember, this was my very first time singing in front of an audience of strangers.

> **Johnny Mohler**   So Bill's up there and he started to sing. Nothing came out. I mean nothing, he froze. The piano player tried to jump in to help, but as hard as Bill tried *nothing* came out. I hauled ass out of there. I got through the back door and I'm running through the parking lot and here comes Medley right behind me, cussing me out all the way. But we got in the car and on the way home Bill told me, "Mohler, I am gonna be a singer. I know I got scared and nothing came out and I froze, but I am gonna be a singer." That was the start, that's what really got him going.

That left me back at Fiduccia's Gas Station with my buddies. That's where we hung out and made our plans for the night. We'd all pitch in twenty-five cents for gas and decide whose car to take cruisin' for chicks. A block away was where the bus would pick up Marines to take them to the El Toro Marine base in Orange County. We had a lot of fights with the Marines, and we lost most of them. It's a good thing I pursued music instead of boxing.

Don Fiduccia played a little rhythm guitar and asked me if I'd sing a song he wrote. He said, "I know you can sing and I want to hear somebody sing this song." That changed my life. Pretty soon I was sitting at my mom's piano at home for twelve hours at a time. I taught myself to play Little Richard and Fats Domino songs, stuff like that. People would ask my mom if that drove her nuts, and she'd say, "At least I know where he is." Don and I started driving around picking up chicks by telling them we were the Everly Brothers. Music had gotten hold of me and it's never let go.

Don and I started a group called the Romancers. We'd sing harmony and I began to write songs. Now, I know Les Paul is credited for inventing multi-track recording, but I think I invented it in my Orange County living room. I had two cheap little tape recorders and I'd record with one and then play it back while playing and singing harmony parts and record all that with the other. I'd go back and forth until I had a full group of vocals and piano parts. I had never heard of multi-track recording or Les Paul, I just figured it out. When I produced many of the Righteous Brothers hits I thought back to those days of "producing" multi-track recordings in my living room. What a trip!

My grandpa on my mom's side would watch me doing all this and once told me, "Whatever it is that you're doing there, you're going to make millions someday with this." Whether he was a prophet or just a good guesser, the encouragement sure felt great.

I started knocking on doors trying to sell my songs to established groups. With a mix of youthful bravado and naivety I walked into the office of the fifties hit-making group the Diamonds at 6425 Hollywood Boulevard—I was just nineteen. Their leader Dave Somerville liked my songs enough to actually record two of them.

Dave Somerville   I remember Bill as a nice kid, real skinny and kind of shy. We did two of Bill's songs; one was called "Womaling" and the other "Chimes of My Heart." We released "Womaling," but it didn't chart and then "Chimes of My Heart"

came out as part of our *Best of the Diamonds—
The Mercury Years* collection. In those days you
could just show up and walk into a radio station or
recording studio, and if you had something good
they'd listen.

Soon I wanted to expand beyond what Don and I could do with
just the two of us as the Romancers, so I asked him what he thought
about forming a quartet. That's when the Paramours were born.

2 | The Paramours

The Paramours started as something of an all-Italian group. Don Fiduccia, Sal Fasulo, Nick Tuturro, and me. They called me "Medleyano." We got our first paying gig at Little Italy restaurant in Anaheim. Later Mike Rider joined us on bass guitar, I played piano, Don played rhythm guitar, Sal joined me on the vocals, and Nick was on drums. On Fridays and Saturdays we'd play from nine at night to six in the morning. Nine hours of belting out Little Richard and other pop tunes for $16 a piece and a free dinner—and I loved it.

That's where I first met Bobby Hatfield; he came in to see us with a girl I used to date. Bobby had his group, the Variations, and I had the Paramours. Eventually we added Barry Rillera, who was a killer guitar player. Barry played in both Bobby's group and mine, and he'd always tell me, "You've got to hear this guy Bobby sing." He'd say the same thing to Bobby about me. I went to see Bobby perform, and we became fans of each other.

That's when John Wimber entered the picture. John was a fantastic musician who was playing in Las Vegas regularly, but wanted to come back to Orange County to be closer to his family. Eventually

John became the founder of the worldwide Vineyard Church movement, but at that time he was just trying to put together a great band to play locally.

I knew John even before I knew Bobby. He'd sneak me in to the clubs where his band was playing and late in the evening they'd let me get up and sing some Ray Charles or something like that. He arranged many of the early Righteous Brothers records and, believe it or not, John once asked me what I knew about God.

Even though I'd not always walked the narrow path, my family had been very involved in the Presbyterian Church, and I knew the basics. John was just exploring Christianity, and once he pulled me aside and asked what I knew about the Christian faith. I told him what I knew. Please hear me, I'm not taking any credit for it, but just a few years down the road John was writing all these popular worship songs and starting churches all over the world. Until the day he died I always loved and respected John. He was one of the few guys I knew who did more than talk the talk, he lived it.

Anyway, back in Orange County, John put Bobby, his drummer, me, and Don Fiduccia together and we kept the name the Paramours. We went to work at a club called John's Black Derby and it was like a party. I'd just take off singing and Bobby would grab that harmony note above me and we'd go. As it turned out Bobby and I both spent our teen years trying to tune in a radio station called KGFJ, which barely reached south of Los Angeles. The main DJ was Hunter Hancock and they played all black music—we loved it.

When it came time for Bobby and me to sing we did those songs, it was what we knew. We weren't trying to sound black, we just loved those songs. We were singing rhythm and blues, which really wasn't being done—not by white guys.

We also started doing some of my original songs. I'd written a song called "Little Latin Lupe Lu," which was inspired by this girl I'd met in beauty school, Lupe Laguna. Ray Maxwell, who owned Moonglow Records, came in to see us one night because I'd done some background vocal recording for him. I asked him to listen to "Little Latin Lupe Lu" because the audience really seemed to dig it.

"Let's record it," he said, and we did—me and Bobby and some of his studio guys. When Bobby and I went in to record we were just two guys from the Paramours, and because it was a duet we tried to think of a different name. We thought about the Medfields, the Hatleys and a few others. They didn't click. Finally we landed on a name. Here is the real story of how Bobby and I became the Righteous Brothers.

At that time, Orange County was about the whitest place in the country, but all these black Marines from El Toro Marine base heard that there were these two guys singing rhythm and blues, so they came down to hear us.

In those days if you really liked something, like a great shirt, a white guy would have said, "Boy, that's cool" or "bitchin'," but a black guy would say, "That's righteous, that's a righteous lookin' shirt." And if they liked you as a friend they'd call you a "brother." Like, "Hey brother, how you doin'?"

A lot of times we'd be coming to work and pass one of the black Marines, and he'd say, "Hey righteous brother, how you doin'?" I loved that and so did Bobby. Sometimes at the end of our songs they'd yell out, "That's righteous, brother!" I always thought it would have been better if they'd have yelled out, "That's Beatles, brother!"

Finally, I think it was Bobby who said, "What about the name that the Marines have been callin' us, the black guys. How about the

Righteous Brothers?" I said, "Oh man, I would love that." That was it—we put it on the record. That's the true story, the black Marines from El Toro Marine base named us.

3 | The Rendezvous Ballroom

To say "Little Latin Lupe Lu" was a flop would be an understatement. It didn't fly off the shelves in the record stores; it never even got on the shelves. That is until Mike Patterson came into the picture. Mike Patterson was a great musician who had a killer band that played at the Rendezvous Ballroom in Balboa, California. The Rendezvous had been the place where all the great big bands of the 1930s and 1940s played—Glenn Miller, Benny Goodman, Tommy Dorsey, and the like.

In 1963 the Rendezvous was giving birth to the surf music craze with pioneers like Dick Dale and the Deltones and the Surftones. We'd gotten fired from the Black Derby and Mike begged us to come down and play "Little Latin Lupe Lu." He'd played piano on the recording, and was sure it would go over.

> **Mike Patterson** I used to go to the Black Derby to see them because I knew Bill from school. They just blew me away. I talked to the people at the Rendezvous and told them we needed to get Bill and Bobby down there because I knew the kids would go nuts. Bobby didn't want to do it because

all they would pay was $50 a piece and we argued for about a week.

I told them they'd be in front of 2,000 kids and they could give "Lupe Lu" away. The ones who didn't get a free record would go out and buy it. Finally they gave in and did it. Bill got it, he's always been smart as a whip—it's like he can see into the future.

The truth is, if Patterson didn't come and get us at that point Bobby and I would have gone our separate ways. Thankfully we didn't and we were on fire when we hit the stage at the Rendezvous. We did our rhythm and blues, shouting and screaming, getting down on our knees—these white kids had never seen anything like it.

They went nuts! They probably wondered, "What the hell is this and why do we like it so much?" They didn't know it was OK to feel that way. Up to that point their world was filled with good-looking teen idols like Frankie Avalon and Fabian. Bobby and I didn't consider ourselves good looking, at least not like that, so we weren't afraid to sweat and let it all hang out. We'd been playing to the over-twenty-one crowd at John's Black Derby, and these kids were all just seventeen or eighteen.

It turned out "Lupe Lu" was perfect for them because the beat went really well with this dance they did called "the Surfer Stomp." They'd ask us where they could get a copy, and we told them we'd recorded it, just go down to the record store and order it. They came back the next night and said the record store didn't have any and didn't know how to get it.

So, Bobby and Mike Patterson went to Moonglow Records, got a stack of singles, and took them to Gracie's Music Store in Santa Ana. They said, "Here—if you sell them you sell them, if you don't, use them as Frisbees." The next weekend we told the kids they could buy them there.

In those days in Los Angeles and Orange County there were two big radio stations the kids listened to—KRLA and KFWB. They'd call around to different record stores to see what was selling and those were the records they'd play. They called Gracie's and, as I've heard the story, Gracie herself told them, "Let's see, we've sold nine Elvis songs, four Everly Brothers, but we've sold 1,500 copies of some song called "Little Latin Lupe Lu" by the Righteous Brothers. That's 1,500 in one week."

The KRLA guy said, "Send it up to me." That week on a recorded promo for an upcoming disc jockey record hop they used "Little Latin Lupe Lu" as the background music. The minute the first promo spot aired their phone lines went crazy. "What's that song playing in the background?" I know this sounds like the plot of a bad Elvis movie, but it's true. The disc jockeys started playing the record and that's how the Righteous Brothers were born.

"Lupe Lu" took off like crazy. Right away Ray Maxwell from Moonglow said we needed to do an album. John Wimber arranged all the parts and I got my first taste of being a producer. I didn't even know what a producer was. John wrote down the notes I had in my head and our first album, *The Righteous Brothers—RIGHT NOW!*, was a big hit on the West Coast.

All of a sudden it was packed wherever we performed; I mean you couldn't get in. Even Elvis and his guys came to see us at a little bowling alley in Carolina Pines.

Elvis' friend and radio/TV personality
George Klein   I would schedule my vacations so I could be with Elvis when he was making a movie,

I actually had small parts in eight of them. One time I flew into LAX, and when they picked me up I said, "Where are we going in Hollywood tonight, who are we going to see?" We'd always go see the best shows and see the biggest stars. They said, "We ain't going to Hollywood tonight. See that little bowling alley over there? That's where we're going, there are some entertainers there you've got to see GK."

"Oh, man, I ain't going to no damn bowling alley tonight! C'mon man, let's go down to Hollywood."

"No, that's where we're going."

So we go in, and man, they sang their asses off. Coming from the South I'd seen a lot of soul singers, but never two white guys who could sing like that. You could tell they weren't faking it—it was for real. We went backstage and I asked, "Are you guys from Mississippi or Georgia or someplace like that?"

"No, we're from Orange County, California."

I was thinking, how the hell did they get all that soul? That was the start of our lifetime friendship.

We were like kids in a candy store—young, dumb and full of rum. We didn't take anything seriously because we didn't work hard at it, it just happened. Really, what were the odds of this happening? Little Moonglow Records out of Garden Grove, California, records these two white guys who sound black, and they get a hit the first time out.

We were enough of a hit that Atlantic Records, led by the legendary Ahmet Ertegun, picked up the national distribution rights for "Lupe Lu" and that's where the term "blue-eyed soul" really came from. Atlantic was pretty much an all-black, R&B label. When their public relations guy Red Schwartz took us out to promote it on radio stations, we found that most of them were black stations. In those days, radio was really divided like that.

Unfortunately, Atlantic forgot to mention that we were white. When we showed up to do interviews, they were stunned. They'd still do the interview, but when we left, they'd quit playing the record. It wasn't a racial thing. It was like "we play black artists." Other stations just played opera or bluegrass—they were just staying true to their formats.

Of course when "Lovin' Feelin'" came around, they said, "Screw it, these guys are black. They're black enough." One DJ in Philadelphia started saying, "Here's my blue-eyed soul brothers." In the 1950s and 1960s black guys would use the term "blue-eye" to refer to a white guy. He was hipping his audience to the fact that we were two white guys. It was like a secret code and it caught on.

Our second album was titled *Some Blue-Eyed Soul*. After that any white guy who was singing so-called black music was considered a "blue-eyed soul singer." It kind of bothers me when other singers call themselves "blue-eyed soul" because we didn't give ourselves that name. Black people named us that, and you don't just walk around giving yourself that title. Throughout my career I've always felt embraced by R&B/Soul music artists and fans . . . and the feeling is more than mutual.

4 | The Double-Whammy

In the sixties there were two things that could really derail a young man's music career, getting drafted and getting married. I managed to do both. Just as "Lupe Lu" was really taking off I got my draft notice. Because of my nerves, my draft classification was 1Y. I don't know what the hell that is, but I think it means somebody you don't want to be in a foxhole with. Apparently they only took 1Y guys if they ran out of everybody else.

About the same time, my girlfriend Karen got pregnant and we decided to get married. Sadly, because of all the pressure surrounding my career, Karen ended up miscarrying. Being away all the time put a lot of strain on our marriage, it was really hard for her. Later in the book, I'm going to take the time to properly introduce you to Karen, she was one of the greatest things that ever happened to me. Believe me; she's worth getting to know. Her life and tragic death changed me forever.

The pressure was swallowing me too. Even though we were getting really hot we wondered if this rock & roll thing was just a fad. Bobby and I used to talk about maybe saving some of the money we were making, but we really didn't. Thankfully it wasn't a fad. I'm still singing "Lupe Lu" after all these years, and people still go crazy for it.

One of the reasons I think we lasted so long, beyond the string of hit records, is that we understood that the live performances had to be more than just us standing there singing. It was a show. We were a generation behind the Frank Sinatra, Dean Martin, Jerry Lewis, Sammy Davis crowd, but we took pages out of their books. Our shows were high-energy and funny. I was more the straight man and Bobby was the cut-up.

Comedian/actor Brad Garrett (who opened for the Righteous Brothers for many years)

Bobby could have been a stand-up comedian. He was literally one of the funniest, quickest people I'd ever met. We really had a lot of fun. I think Bill and Bobby lasted so well because they, like Dean Martin and Jerry Lewis, were very different people. They were really funny together.

We were working all the time, perfecting our act, but we still couldn't take ourselves too seriously. We followed "Lupe Lu" with other West Coast hits, "Justine," "Koko Joe," and "My Babe," but still considered ourselves something of a regional act, although "Justine," and "Koko Joe," helped us get our first movie roles in one of those beachball era flicks called *A Swingin' Summer*. We were California "hot" and these were California movies. It wasn't *Gone with the Wind*, but it featured us and other popular musical acts of the day— Gary Lewis and the Playboys, the Rip Chords, and the Dovells. James Stacy was the star. Ironically, he was married to Connie

Stevens at the time, who later became my long-time girlfriend. You'll hear from her later in the book.

What I probably remember best about it was that it was Raquel Welch's first movie; she played the role of "Jeri." I'll never forget this; I was standing back from the cameras and this secretary, very proper and professional with glasses and a modest dress, walks on to the set and starts talking to this guy. All of a sudden the music starts and she takes her glasses off, undoes her hair, and goes into this incredible dance. I had no idea they were filming, it was my first time on a movie set. That was my introduction to Raquel Welch; let's just say I noticed her.

We were working all the time and making good money, but we were just a couple of young kids enjoying the ride. We felt like we were getting away with murder. We were getting paid like $600 a night to get up there and do what we'd have paid them to let us do.

All that was about to change.

5 | The Beatles

The early 1960s was a confusing time in American music. Top 40 radio was becoming the hot format, playing songs from the forty most popular listed in *Billboard* magazine. It was crazy; you'd hear a song by Elvis or Fats Domino followed by something from Louis Armstrong or Perry Como. Generations of musical taste were at war, fighting for space on the crowded AM radio dial.

Suddenly, in 1964, a musical lightning bolt reached across the Atlantic. These four guys from England, who didn't look or sound like anything we'd ever heard, took over. The British musical invasion began and we were asked to come along for the ride.

We were baffled. Why are these English guys asking us to be on their first American tour? How do they even know who we are? As it turned out, our first two albums had become kind of cultish for "garage bands" in England because we were white guys who sounded black, which they really loved. Even though we didn't know a lot about the Beatles, we soon found out they knew a lot about us.

On the tour plane, George Harrison came back to ask, "Who took that guitar solo on your record 'My Babe'?" He thought it was the guitar player from the Bill Black Combo, who was on the tour too. I told him no, it was our guitar player, Barry Rillera, who was with us on the plane. So before you know it, George is a few seats over, picking Barry's brain asking, "How did you do that?" Barry taught him about using banjo strings to bend notes and other cool guitar techniques. Sure enough, on the next Beatles album, there was George, trying some Barry Rillera stuff.

We were all just young kids, so we got to know them pretty well. John and Paul especially were goofy, Ringo was funny but a little more serious, and George was very serious. George was a real musical guy—John and Paul were just extremely gifted.

On the plane they were very "teenage-like." They were as knocked out with what was happening as everybody else. I watched a lot of their interviews, and they were a little like Bobby Hatfield. They would never answer anything straight, they were always jokin' around.

The one unbelievable thing I remember about the Beatles tour was that whenever one of the other opening acts, like Jackie DeShannon, was having a little throat trouble or something, the Beatles' manager Brian Epstein would come to us and ask, "Guys, can you do one more song?" We ended up doing about forty minutes. We were the last act on before the Beatles, and these poor thirteen- and fourteen-year-old screaming, crying little girls didn't know they were gonna have to live through an hour and a half of crap before they saw them. We never really took offense to them yelling, "We want the Beatles." Of course they did!

Altogether we did around fifty dates with them. Many of these concerts were in outdoor stadiums, and they'd put this fence up about ten or twenty feet in front of the stage, and all these kids out on the field were being crushed against the fence. So we're singing and watching nurses haul people out of there because they were being crushed. That was just a really odd feeling and very dangerous. I mean, you've got like 40,000 kids on the field with a fence, and they're all trying to push to the front. It was scary.

I think the most amazing thing about the Beatles tour was this. The minute the Beatles went on, for some reason they turned on all the lights in the auditorium or stadium. I thought, "How weird," because they weren't on when we or any of the other acts were on. We just had the normal spotlights and concert stage lighting. I wondered if they just wanted it all lit up so they could see everybody. So I asked somebody why.

They said, "No, we're not turning the lights on at all. It's flashbulbs." Camera flashbulbs lit the place up, I mean full on lit up until they were offstage. It was like the lights were on. But it was flashbulbs.

Toward the end of the Beatles tour we asked to leave early because we'd gotten a call to be part of a new TV experiment, a weekly teen music show that would air across the country. We didn't really know what we were signing up for, but we soon learned about the incredible power of TV. We flew back to Los Angeles to tape the pilot of *Shindig*.

6 | *Shindig*

Pat and Lolly Vegas were brothers and a great duo, a lot like Bobby and me. We went to see their show and they asked us to come up to sing. After we finished, Jack Good, who was the producer of *Shindig*, approached us. He was there to see Pat and Lolly, but decided he wanted us for the show. He said they started filming March 1st, and we shrugged and said, "Unfortunately, we're going to be on tour with four new guys from England then."

Thankfully, we decided to leave the tour early and came home to start *Shindig*. In 1964, with just three major networks, a hit show would have more viewers than *American Idol* does today. We had no idea what that meant. All we knew was it was a cool show, full of high energy, where we really got to let it hang out. We were just doing the same thing we'd done at the Black Derby—screaming, sweating, throwing the microphone back and forth; we had no clue about how it would change our lives.

We got a call from our agent who said they wanted us to do a show in Chicago. "Who wants us to do a show in Chicago?" Some radio station wanted us and we couldn't figure out why. We knew that people in California were watching the show and digging it, but

Chicago? We said OK, but it was the first time we'd ever headlined a show outside of California.

When we showed up there we saw huge billboards with the Righteous Brothers in giant letters on the top. We stopped at a gas station outside of Chicago and when we went in to pay for the gas the guy said, "You guys are the Righteous Brothers!" That blew our minds.

"How do you know us?"

"I watch *Shindig* every week," he said with excitement.

When we walked out on stage the kids went nuts, standing and screaming before we ever sang a note. We didn't understand what it meant to be in people's homes every week; they felt like they knew us. It was kind of scary and really exciting at the same time.

Even though *Shindig* was filmed, it was probably the closest thing to a live performance you could get. The audience was filled with frenzied teens, and Jack Good kept it moving like a live show to keep the energy up. Once we started we didn't stop. Sometimes the dancers would only have thirty seconds or so to change between numbers, they were great. The band was unbelievable—Billy Preston, Leon Russell, Larry Knechtel, James Burton, and just about every other hot studio musician in Los Angeles. And the backup singers, especially the Blossoms featuring Darlene Love, were great too. That's where I first met Darlene, who eventually became another one of my longtime girlfriends. Yes, I was blazing a trail in race relations and didn't even know it by dating a black woman. You'll hear much more about that later as well.

One guy they could never get on *Shindig* was Elvis, but they really wanted him. Because he'd become a Righteous Brothers fan and friend, he'd call Jack Good and make requests for us to perform certain songs. What Elvis wanted, Elvis got, but they never got him to perform on the show. I guess his manager, Colonel Tom Parker, thought it wasn't right for him.

Shindig gave us the opportunity to meet and perform with the biggest stars in pop music. That's where I first met Brian Wilson and the Beach Boys. I'm embarrassed to say that Bobby and I thought the Beach Boys' early stuff, the surfin' stuff, was kinda "bubble-gummy." It certainly wasn't Ray Charles or Wilson Pickett, who we loved.

That all changed for me in the ABC-TV studio men's restroom when the Beach Boys were guests on *Shindig*. Brian was a big fan of Phil Spector, who we'd just started working with. He came to me and said, "Bill, I'm Brian Wilson of the Beach Boys. I want you to hear something."

I said, "OK," and he took me to the men's restroom at ABC where they actually had a piano. Nothin' better than that, man. That reverb in there . . . that's the verb you've been lookin' for all your life! Brian sat down at the piano and said, "I want you to hear something that me and the group do."

I'm thinking, "Oh brother," but I said, "Yeah sure, go ahead."

Brian was a big fan of the vocal group the Four Freshmen, who were famous for their tight, precise harmonies. So Brian and the others go into the Four Freshmen version of "The Lord's Prayer" with Brian's arrangement.

I sat there stunned. Not just, "Wow," I mean I was stunned. I had thought these guys only played bubblegum surf music, and they were doing something I couldn't do with a shotgun. I couldn't do that real tight harmony, but Bobby could. I said, "Hang on a minute," and I went and got Bobby.

"C'mon, you gotta hear the Beach Boys. Believe me—you'll thank me later." I knew it was mostly Brian, because he was showing them all what to do, but I also knew the other guys were awfully damn good because they were able to do what he was telling them to do. It was all out of Brian's head, but they were capable of pulling it off. My respect for them immediately went zoom.

Brian was the soul of the Beach Boys. His brother Carl, who was just the sweetest man in the world, was the heart. Carl was soft and gentle. When you hear him sing "God Only Knows," you can just tell. The last time I saw Carl was in Vegas, shortly before he passed away in 1998, and he'd brought his mom. He was wheeling her around in a wheelchair everywhere, even backstage. He was that kind of guy. You loved him the minute you met him.

But Brian was the soul. I really got to know Brian when I was recording at Western Studios. There was a big studio that I was recording in because I'd be working with orchestras. Brian would often be recording next door in the smaller studio. We were always there late at night—this was before Brian had his episodes and his problems. He was just a very normal kid, but you could tell he was very sensitive. He'd come in the studio and say, "Bill, would you come in and listen to something for a minute? I feel something's wrong." And I'd go over and give my opinion.

Sometimes I'd grab him and say, "Brian, come in here a minute— what's wrong here?" and he'd give me his opinion. We became really good friends. I probably shouldn't say this but Brian thought my voice was "it." He loved Bobby too, but he really thought my voice was incredible—what a compliment. And when he found out I'd produced *Soul and Inspiration*, it freaked him out.

He still calls me about once a month. Actually my friend Jeff Foskett, who's Brian's right-hand man, calls and says, "Bill, it's Jeff. I've got somebody here who wants to talk to you." Then Brian comes on. "Hey Bill, how you doin'?" Every time I talk to him he asks me the same thing, "Did you produce *Soul and Inspiration*?"

I say, "Yep."

He says, "Man, what a great record, we do that every day at sound check," and they do.

Since Carl Wilson passed away, they have a cancer benefit every year, and one time Brian asked me to come down. He told Jeff Foskett to ask me if I'd do "Lovin' Feelin'" with him, and I told Jeff I'd be happy to. But apparently, they started rehearsing it, and Brian slammed down the piano and said, "Nope. I'm not gonna do it. I'm too scared."

When I got there that night, he told me, "Bill, I'm sorry, but I'm just too scared to sing with you." I said, "Brian, you don't need to sing with me, but you should never feel that way. I'm in awe of you."

He said, "Well, I can't help it."

Eventually I did get to sing with him. In 2007, I recorded one of my best albums, *Damn Near Righteous*. One of the cuts is a song I've always wanted to record; the classic Beach Boys tune "In My Room," with vocals by me, Phil Everly, and Brian Wilson.

I was really concerned about him last year when the Beach Boys went out on their reunion tour; I mean I love the guy a lot. Jeff Foskett would call every few days and tell me how things were going. Apparently, at least during the tour, everyone got along fine, and Brian was feeling great and having fun again. That was so good to hear. Part of my heart hopes Brian can someday recapture that innocent joy I saw when I met him in the *Shindig* bathroom . . . he's a giant talent and a giant guy.

As *Shindig* exploded we found ourselves performing for larger and larger crowds. At the time, the Cow Palace in San Francisco was *the* giant West coast venue for the hottest acts; we'd played there with the Beatles. Now we were coming back as a featured act. That's where we met Phil Spector and he hatched an idea that took us to the moon.

7 | The Cow Palace

I'll never forget their names—Tom Donahue and Bob Mitchell. They were the most popular disc jockeys in San Francisco; I mean they owned the town. They'd throw these huge shows at the Cow Palace with maybe fifteen acts. It was like the Yellow Pages of rock & roll and they asked us to come. We did a bunch of shows there.

There was always a big fight between the artists about who went on when. Most of the acts wanted to close the show, but not us. We always wanted to go on third. They'd say, "Oh no, we need you guys for the closing spot." We said no. We knew the audience was going to be fresh, and we wanted to get done and go to the bar anyway. By the time the fourteenth or fifteenth act came on, those kids were worn out. Once Jan and Dean, who we knew from Orange County, dug in their heels and demanded to close the show. Our response was, "OK, we don't care," and we really didn't. Later I think they were really sorry they'd made that demand; even teenagers have a limit to how much they can take in.

One time Phil Spector was conducting the band. His group, the Ronettes, was on the show and he got it in his mind that he was going to make records with the Righteous Brothers.

We were still on Moonglow Records, and they had two more years on our contract. Phil called them and said, "Listen, I'd like to lease the remainder of the Righteous Brothers' contract."

When Moonglow told us, we said, "I don't know, Phil Spector makes these girl records, "Da Doo Ron Ron" and all these great hits, but that's not where we're comin' from." I asked my friend Nino Tempo, who had big hits with his sister April Stevens, what he thought.

He said, "Man, he'll make you hit records."

So we went up to Chateau Marmont to meet Phil. He said, "I have this song for you." He had asked Barry Mann and Cynthia Weil to write us a song, and they wrote "You've Lost That Lovin' Feelin'." Why they wrote that song for us I'll never know. I mean, if they'd listened to any of our stuff it didn't fit. They wrote it as kind of like a bouncy sing-along.

Barry Mann   I always liked "Baby I Need Your Lovin'," which was a hit song out at that time by the Four Tops. I thought Bill and Bobby would sound great on a ballad like that with those emotional R&B qualities to it.

Cynthia Weil   Phil Spector told us, "This will be one of the most important songs you've ever had." I responded, "Any song with 'Whoa, whoa, whoa' in it can't be that important!" Coming from a musical theater background I guess I was kind of a musical snob. I didn't really have an audio vision for how the record would turn out, but the amazing thing about Spector was that he'd get something

in his head and then go in and reproduce that
sound. The song was ours, but the record was really
his creation.

Barry and Phil sat down at the piano and started to play and sing it. They both had high, thin voices and they sang it about four keys higher than we eventually recorded it. I said, "That sounds like a great song for the Everly Brothers," and it would have been a great song for them—they were one of the few white groups I liked. The Everly Brothers, Dion and the Belmonts, and Elvis were huge with me.

They said, "No, no, just give it a shot." We did, but I couldn't hit the high, emotional notes. I think it started in F and we kept lowering the key, lowering the key, until we finally got down to C. When it started off with that deep "You never close your eyes anymore when I kiss your lips," it took on this whole different emotional feel. Phil told Barry to slow it down a little, and then we were ready to go into the studio.

Now, Phil was very sane, but he wanted people to think he was very eccentric. He wanted that image and he did things to build it. One time we were at his house rehearsing with Carole King, and all of a sudden the lights went down low and there was this howling from outside the window, almost like a wolf but we could tell it wasn't. Phil had planned the whole thing and gotten some guy to stand outside the window and howl. Why? Good question; it was bizarre.

He'd also throw an occasional tantrum in an airport or restaurant. Once he made a big scene in a restaurant because they asked him to take off his hat. I think he didn't want to reveal his hairpiece or something.

But, for the most part, when we were with him he was fine. When we were rehearsing "Lovin' Feelin'," Bobby asked him, "What am I supposed to do when Medley's singin' this song?"

Phil said, "Go to the bank!"

He was brilliant in the studio. You only have to listen to "Lovin' Feelin'" today and know that it was recorded on two or three tracks to know that he was a genius. When Phil did the music tracks he wouldn't let anybody in the studio except us. Bobby could have been there but chose not to come. But I was there and I was like a sponge, soaking up everything I could. He wouldn't let anyone else in the engineer booth because he didn't want any other producer to know how he was doing what he did.

After the music track was finished, when it came time for Bobby and me to put our voices on, all of a sudden the booth got packed. Keith Richards, Mick Jagger, and all kinds of other celebrities and record business giants were there. This was Phil's time, his party to show off his talent. We'd be singing, and in the booth they were all joking, talking, and laughing—it was incredibly distracting. After about three hours we called Phil out and said, "We'll be back tomorrow at six."

He said, "We're not done."

"We'll come back tomorrow, and please don't have anybody in the studio."

He just said, "OK."

We came back the next day to an empty studio and recorded what is now the most-played song in the history of American radio. According to BMI, the music licensing agency that tracks this stuff, no recording by Elvis, the Beatles, or anyone else has been played as often on American radio, ever. It's pretty cool to be part of that.

At first, none of us thought it was a hit. When Phil played it for Barry Mann over the phone, Barry yelled, "Phil, Phil, you've got it on the wrong speed!" He thought it was being mistakenly played at 33⅓ instead of 45 rpm—and so did some of the distributors.

But the record started to take off. We went to England to promote it, because the song had also been recorded there by the British pop star Cilla Black. Not that we wanted to, but our version just knocked hers out of the box. That's where we reconnected with her manager Brian Epstein, who we knew from when we went on tour with the Beatles. We really liked Brian; we thought he was a great guy. He couldn't have been nicer on the Beatles' tour; he kept track of the opening acts, asking if we were OK, or if we needed anything.

While we were on that tour he actually asked if he could manage us, but the Beatles, England, and all that was so foreign to us we said no thanks. Still, we thought Brian was a really sweet and level guy, even in the middle of all the Beatles madness.

When we got back to New York, Phil put us together with Barry and Cynthia again to write the follow-up song. They wrote "(You're My) Soul and Inspiration." Somehow, some way, something happened, and I still don't know what or why. Phil said, "No, we're not gonna do that song. We're going back to California to work with this young girl songwriter Carole King."

The song Phil and Carole had for us was "Just Once in My Life," which turned out to be a top ten hit. Even though it didn't quite reach the success of some of our other songs, "Just Once in My Life" is a phenomenal record, maybe better than "Lovin' Feelin'." Fortunately, I did eventually reconnect with Barry and Cynthia, and a few years later I produced "Soul and Inspiration," which went to number one.

After "Just Once in My Life," Phil came to me and said he wanted to produce the singles, and he wanted me to produce the albums. He'd spend way too much time and way too much money producing all the cuts. Phil was real good with us, and the only reason we left him was some legal and financial issue with Moonglow, the company he'd leased our contract from. Moonglow said he couldn't record with us.

I didn't want to leave him. Working with Phil was a blessing to me. This guy was making some of the greatest records in the world. I loved going in the studio with him and the best songwriters in the world and making these incredible recordings.

Of course Phil's troubles later in his life are pretty well known. I don't know what really happened with that 2003 shooting at his house (with Lana Clarkson) and this is only my speculation, but if he'd just said, "It was an accident," I think people would have believed him. I think his ego was such that he didn't want to take any responsibility. "She committed suicide" just didn't make any sense. I think his ego jumped up and got in the way.

I wasn't sure if we'd get to work with Phil again, and then our agent, Jerry Perenchio, met with MGM. They offered us a million dollars cash and said they'd take care of the legal mess with Moonglow. We went for it. Still, if it was just up to me, I would have turned all that down to stay with Phil.

With the deal Jerry made for us and "Lovin' Feelin'" zooming up the charts, we were entering a whole new world. It was everything I'd dreamed of, but it was way beyond Bobby's comfort zone. When you go from "Lupe Lu" hot to "Lovin' Feelin'" hot, everything in your world changes. Everybody wants a piece of you, and it really affected us. Thankfully, Jerry Perenchio and David Cohen, whom you'll meet a bit later, were there to protect and guide us.

Even if you aren't familiar with the name Jerry Perenchio, you've likely been touched by his life—I know I have and still am. He's become a huge media mogul and giant player in the entertainment industry, but he's still the same sweet guy I knew way back when. Remember the mansion TV's *Beverly Hillbillies* lived in? That's Jerry's house—and he owns the mansions on both sides of it too. He owned the Spanish-language TV network Univision, and was the first guy to do pay-per-view boxing when he promoted the 1971 "Fight of the Century" between Muhammad Ali and Joe Frazier. TV shows like *All in the Family*, *Maude*, and *Diff'rent Strokes* were all produced by Jerry's company. To me, he's like a big brother figure and remains one of my closest friends and advisors.

How Jerry became our agent is an interesting story.

Jerry Perenchio   I was in the talent agency business and all of our clients were middle-of-the-road acts like Andy Williams and Johnny Mathis. Rock & roll was coming in and one of the young gals in my office said, "Mr. P if we don't get into the rock & roll business we're not gonna be in business, we've got to sign some rock & roll acts." I said, "Go get me a *Billboard* magazine." She did and I opened it and saw that the #1 record in the country was "You've Lost That Lovin' Feelin'" by the Righteous Brothers. I told her to go get the record and I listened and thought it was sensational. I told her to find out where they were performing. They happened to be playing at the Cow Palace outside of San Francisco, and they were doing an afternoon show with Phil Spector and a then-unknown act, Sonny and Cher.

I went to the show and liked them very much. They were staying at a crummy little motel near there and I met with them before their evening show and said, "I want to represent you, I think I could do a hell of a job. Who are you signed with now?" They told me General Artists Corporation (GAC), which made it a little painful because I used to work for GAC. I told them to fire their agent and sign with me; I really had my "selling light" on. I'm not sure how excited Bobby was about it, but Bill seemed very interested. Later that day they told me they wanted to do it and I helped them fire their agent.

That's how I came to represent the Righteous Brothers. They were just terrific guys. Bill and I hit it off right away; Bobby was always a little more stand-offish. Bill seemed to be the more mature one—we've been friends ever since.

Even back then Jerry really understood the complex relationship between Bobby and me. He "got" me, through all my quietness and social anxiety he always believed in me. That gave me a lot of confidence. Jerry and Bobby never really hit it off. When Bobby got married, Jerry threw him an incredible wedding reception at the Beverly Hills Hotel. Everybody who was anybody in the music business was there and it was such a big deal that the then-popular TV show *Hollywood Backstage* covered it. You can watch the whole thing on YouTube, just type in "Righteous Brothers Hollywood

Backstage." Jerry laid out fifty grand for it, that's $50,000 in the mid-sixties. He never got a thank you from Bobby. I don't believe Bobby was being rude on purpose, that's just how he was—but I think it hurt Jerry.

Jerry got us a great opportunity to be the opening act for comedian Jack Benny in Lake Tahoe. Young people today probably don't even know who Jack Benny was, but in the 1960s Jack was still a show business superstar. Radio, movies, TV—Jack Benny was one of those instantly recognizable voices and faces of comedy.

As part of the package they wanted us to do a comedy sketch with Jack. We went to his office and his writers gave us the script and we went through it. The next thing you know Jerry Perenchio gets a call from Jack Benny's office saying, "We don't think the tall guy can pull this off. The little guy's OK, but the big one—he's too bashful and laid back."

Jerry countered, "Call me the night after they open and tell me if the guy cut it or not."

The night after we opened he got the call, "Man, they killed it." (*killed it* in the good, show-biz sense). For some reason, Jerry always had a blind belief in me. As I've said, he was like my big brother, and no matter what he always looked out for me. Even when I'd buy a house or car he'd check it out first to make sure I wasn't getting screwed. I can't say enough good things about Jerry. A couple of years ago I had dinner with him at his house and got to tell him what he really meant to me.

"You believed in me when you didn't have to and maybe shouldn't have. You took chances and that gave me so much confidence."

He cried. That's who Jerry Perenchio is.

One great thing Jerry did when he took over our act was to introduce us to David Cohen. To this day David is one of my closest friends and advisors. Jerry said, "The first thing you need is a business manager, someone to handle your money." Julius Lefkowitz & Co. was one of the big show-business management firms and Jerry didn't like the first guy they put us with so they had David Cohen take over our account.

David is a Jewish, New York-born accounting guy and I didn't quite know what to make of him. I'll never forget our first conversation. I was on the road and I called him and said, "David, this is Bill Medley of the Righteous Brothers, I need some bread, and I need it right away."

He paused and asked, "Bread?"

After a while I figured out he probably wondered why I didn't just go to the grocery store. He didn't understand I was asking for money. I finally explained what I wanted, but it made me nervous. As it turned out David was a great business manager. He paid all of our bills, and for years he gave me an allowance of just $60 a week, and that was more than enough. A lot of what I have today is there because David took care of my money. For almost fifty years he's been by my side through the good times and the bad.

From his very first meeting with me and Bobby he became our "mediator," managing our different personalities and needs. I love the guy. Go figure, an Orange County Protestant and a New York Jew. David used to joke about not being sure they even let Jews into Orange County. He'd call me from Los Angeles and say, "I'm coming down, raise the Orange curtain."

David Cohen   Bill called me on Christmas week in 1966. He said, "I need to talk with you, where can we meet?"

We met at a restaurant called Frascati's over on Sunset. Remember, I was the only Jewish person Bill knew in those years. Bill sat down and said, "Are you covered?"

"Am I what?"

"Look, I know you're Jewish, and I know the religion. If you die do I have to go to Jesus to take care of you or have you got somebody? Are you covered?"

I told him I was covered and that's when I realized that he cared deeply about me. In those days Bill hardly said a word to anyone, but he drove all the way up from Orange County just to ask if I was OK. That's when we really became friends.

8 | We're, uh, *I'm* Off to New York

In 1965 "Lovin' Feelin'" was the #1 record in the country, and that brought offers from everywhere. Murray the K was the biggest disc jockey in New York at that time, and he'd put on these huge shows at the Brooklyn Fox Theater. Five shows a day with the hottest radio stars in the country.

Bobby didn't want to do it. He hurt his back; he had back problems his whole life. And as I've said, our comfort levels were just miles apart. Everything that was happening to us seemed to overwhelm him. So, we told Murray the K we couldn't do it. He said, "You *will* do it or I'll sue you." He'd promised his audiences that the act with the #1 song in the country was going to be there.

I said, "OK, I'll do it alone." Our band leader Mike Patterson and I got on a plane and went to New York. Our agent Jerry Perenchio, wanting to make sure we relaxed I guess, sent a couple of hookers up to our room. Being the nice guys we are and not wanting to refuse their hospitality, we took advantage of the situation. Again—young, dumb, and full of rum. That was our first experience in New York.

41

It was incredible. Five shows a day . . . it was me and the Motown galaxy of stars. In between shows I'd sing gospel songs with the Temptations, their bass singer Melvin Franklin and I became really good friends.

In those days there was still quite a racial divide. The daytime audiences were all white but the last two shows at night were all black. Everybody, black and white, loved the Motown artists and "Lovin' Feelin'" was #1 with them all. The band was incredible—two drummers, killer horn section, Martha and the Vandellas opened with their hit "Heat Wave"—the energy was awesome.

What blew me away was the black audience. There were 1,500 packed seats there, and the entire audience sang Bobby's parts! Note for note, riff for riff, they did "Lovin' Feelin'" with me. It sounded like a really hip giant choir. As part of my show I did the song "Ol' Man River." It had a vamp at the end where I'd start doing all my soulful shouting and repeating, "Just keeps rollin', just keeps rollin.'" All of a sudden this black guy stands up and shouts out like he's in church, "Hold it, stop it, I can't take no more!" Wow. One reviewer wrote, "Bill Medley got a standing ovation that they only reserve for Ray Charles." It was sensational, one of the high points of my career.

That experience made me realize I could make it on my own if I had to. It's not that I wanted to. Bobby and I still had much success ahead of us, but I knew I could if I needed to.

9 | Riding the Wave

To say "Lovin' Feelin'" changed my life would be an understatement. It really brought out the differences in me and Bobby. It wasn't a good or bad thing; it was just that we had different comfort zones. I loved riding the wave of success but it was not Bobby's happy place, at least not all the commitments and promotional work.

> **Road manager Mike Patterson** "Lovin' Feelin'" went through the ceiling and it was a whole new era for us. Everything happened so fast, and we became big so quickly. Some nights we'd work in front of 20,000 people. Bill loved it but not Bobby. Bobby hated doing interviews. Once he turned down an interview with *LIFE* magazine, which was huge in those days. Here I am running around trying to get the band and everyone else where they needed to be, and then I have to manage the *LIFE* magazine people waiting in the lobby. I couldn't get Bobby out of his hotel room, he just wasn't interested.

Bobby loved going to the parties and the Hollywood events like the *Grammys*, but I focused all my energy on the music. I loved being in the studio and working on the creative stuff, we were just cut from two different cloths.

Not to say that the pressure didn't affect me, I felt it too. When you get hot everybody needs you—the TV shows, wardrobe fittings, on and on. And, the second I got home Phil Spector had me in the studio working on "Just Once in My Life." Here's a story I never told Bobby and this is the first time I've told it publicly.

After "Lovin' Feelin'" Phil wanted me to leave Bobby. He called me in and said, "We can make a lot of records together." I thought it was because I'd sang so much of the lead on "Lovin' Feelin'" that he thought he could make better records with just one guy; at least that's what he said. The truth is Phil knew he'd created a monster with the Righteous Brothers and he wanted to destroy it. His ego was such that it was important to him that the songs weren't "Righteous Brothers songs" but rather "Phil Spector productions."

"Lovin' Feelin'" had become a Righteous Brothers record and his ego couldn't deal with that. I believe his ego was bigger than his need for money, so he was willing to destroy us, and damn near did. I said, "No, I'm not leaving Bobby, and the next record we do better have Bobby on it a lot more."

I don't know that I turned Phil down so much out of loyalty; at least it didn't feel that way at the time. I think my business brain kicked in and I figured it would be nuts to destroy what we were building. And, I was really proud of what we had done and who we were. I didn't want to walk away from that—no way. I still felt connected to Bobby and I was having a shit-load of fun with him. When we were on the road and performing he was a fun, funny guy to be around. Bobby and I were the Righteous Brothers, end of story.

Unfortunately, the next record, Carole King's "Just Once in My Life"—maybe Phil's best production ever—had even less of Bobby. I really think that was the beginning of our break-up. I can understand why Bobby was pissed off; if things had been reversed I would have been pissed off too.

10 | The Green Light from Sinatra

Jerry Perenchio may be the smartest man I've ever known. Just as "Lovin' Feelin'" was cresting, he called and said Moe Lewis from the Sands Hotel in Las Vegas wanted to come to see us perform. No rock act had ever worked Vegas, at that time it was the land of Sinatra and his crew.

Jerry told us, "I know you can't make the money in Vegas that you can on the one-nighters, but if you go to Vegas it will be the best investment you ever make, because you can always go there to work." He was 150 percent right. Las Vegas saved my life.

When Moe Lewis came to preview the act at a San Jose concert, Jerry told us, "Listen, Moe Lewis is here. Don't say any of those dirty, bullshit jokes—don't do any of that stuff, nothing dirty." Now, we'd just taped *The Danny Kaye Show* earlier that day and had flown in on a private jet—we were exhausted. We walked onstage and the first thing Bobby said was, "We just flew in and we're a couple of tired turds." I could hear Perenchio swallow from the back of the room.

Apparently that didn't turn Moe off too much because he offered us a shot in the lounge at the Sands. We'd be the first rock act ever to invade the Sands, but Moe said there was one thing in the way, "I wanna bring you in, but I've got to get Sinatra's OK first because he's gonna be in the main room then."

I'm sure Frank Sinatra didn't have a clue who the Righteous Brothers were. Rock & roll was a million miles away from swing music and "the Rat Pack." The gap was enormous; I'm sure a lot of those guys thought rock was a piece of shit—loud crap with only three chords. I've never asked her, but I've got to believe Frank's daughter Nancy, who was a good friend of ours, was in the room when they asked for his OK. I can only imagine that conversation.

"Dad, the Righteous Brothers are great, you'll love them."

"OK cookie, you got it."

Not only did Sinatra not know us, the whole town—the dealers, waitresses, nobody knew us . . . Vegas was an island unto itself in those days. When we opened, that changed. We had lines going out of the building waiting to get in to see us. Again, we discovered the power of radio and TV.

We learned that one of the reasons the Sands needed his OK was because Frank always brought in huge parties of his friends whenever he was in Vegas. He'd take them to the lounge after his show and that's where he'd hold court. We always knew when he was coming because, despite the long lines waiting to get in, there was a long row of empty chairs from the stage to the back of the room with a bottle of Jack Daniels at every other chair. It was the heaviest of the heavy-hitters in Hollywood—Burt Lancaster, all the Rat Pack crew, you name it. One night I had to sing "Georgia" with my musical hero Ray Charles sitting four feet from me.

After a few days Moe Lewis and Sands entertainment director Jack Entratter said, "Boys, we're going to take you backstage to get your picture taken with Mr. Sinatra. But, don't say anything, don't do anything—just go in and have your picture taken." They took us in and there was the usual gathering of stars in Frank's dressing room. For the first time, thankfully, Bobby didn't say anything. Moe told Frank we'd like to get a picture with him and he said, "Sure."

Now, we knew we weren't supposed to talk but he started asking me questions, "Hey kid, how you doing, how's the reed?" He was referring to my voice, like a sax player's reed. I told him, "Well, I'm fine, Mr. Sinatra." But I wasn't. I was struggling with the dry "Vegas throat" that singers often complain about; I could hardly speak. So he started to tell me how to take care of my voice in the desert climate, but there was a lot of commotion in the room with all the stars and their friends. Suddenly he called out to his man Jilly Rizzo.

"Jilly, take everybody up to my suite, I'll be there shortly."

Jilly ushered everyone out and Frank Sinatra gave us a forty-five-minute coaching session on taking care of your voice. Why he took a liking to us I don't know, maybe we reminded him of when he was coming up. He told us, "I want to see you guys in the health club tomorrow at five o'clock."

Every major act in town (at least every guy) would be in there in that steam room because they just wanted to be around him. He'd take us in there every day and ask for a status report. "How's the reed doin' kid—any better?" They put eucalyptus on the rocks and it helped, although we smelled like eucalyptus for three months afterwards.

I'll never forget, one time he called me over and started to talk to me while he was putting on his hairpiece. It was the greatest rug in the world; it was short and looked so real, not like the helmets that some guys wore. I told him how cool it looked and he said, "Thanks kid." I thought it was amazing that he'd put it on in front of anybody, let alone me. He was just great to me and his advice about taking care of my voice really helped.

Whenever he'd walk through the casino late at night the whole place would start to buzz. If I was playing blackjack or something he'd make it a point to stop and ask me about my voice and if I needed anything. It was like he was saying to everyone who could hear, "Hey, this is one of my guys, treat him right." I mean, I'm twenty-five years old; it made me feel really special.

I also became good friends with Frank's conductor Quincy Jones; we'd gamble together after our shows. One night Quincy flew this girl in and I'm not sure if it was to be with Frank or not, but she was there for somebody heavy because she was staying in Frank Sinatra's suite. As Quincy was walking her through the casino she saw the sign that said we were in the lounge and told him, "Oh, the Righteous Brothers—I love that tall skinny guy." Next thing you know Quincy comes to get me, "Listen Bill, we brought this girl into town and she's waiting for you in Frank's suite." Again, I have no idea who she was in town to see, but I do know that between our ten and two o'clock shows, while Frank was doing his midnight show, I made my way up to see her. To say we "made love" would be a huge understatement. This girl and I had sex in Frank Sinatra's suite while he was onstage. Am I proud of that? No, I'm just proud I'm still alive. I'm not sure Frank would have appreciated it.

Sometimes people ask me what the difference is between the Vegas of those days and now. I tell them, "There is no difference—the Vegas I knew isn't here anymore." It's like if you tore down your house and built a new one, it just isn't the same house. I like the new Vegas, but it isn't the Vegas I grew up in. It was so exciting and we were just twenty-five years old; we ate it up. We became very aware of the Italian mob guys and we knew the Jewish mob too, because they took care of the casinos. They were great to us; they loved us. When Frank was in the main room they'd always come over after his show because our audiences were filled with unbelievably good-looking twenty-three-year-old girls. We never feared them, although I wouldn't want to be on the wrong side of them either. After a while they started calling us "the Golden Boys" because we were doing such good business.

Another thing that was different about Vegas in those days was the women. Almost every lounge had a topless revue with the most gorgeous women you can imagine. This was long before the days of "boob jobs" and the like, these girls were just naturally, perfectly built. And, there was an understanding among those girls. Every one of them was "kept" by some heavy-hitter movie star or business guy; it was just part of the gig. In fact, most of the cocktail waitresses and other women who worked around the casino were available to the "high-rollers" on demand. Once Jack Entratter asked me, "How ya doin' kid; you been laid lately?" I fumbled around for words and he said, "Go to your room." Five minutes later there's a knock on the door. A beautiful cocktail waitress came in and told me she was sent by Mr. Entratter. Not wanting to disappoint the hotel boss, I received his gracious gift. The thing is, these girls were really great ladies, I mean that. I don't bother much with people I don't like and I got to know a lot of them. They were really sweet. I ran into that cocktail waitress about 20 years later when we were performing in Reno, Nevada. It turns out she became the owner of one of the biggest whorehouses outside of town and she offered me a gift, "Bill, can I send you up someone? Really, they're all beautiful college girls." Being older and wiser I graciously declined, but it took me right back to the 1960s in Vegas.

Once I was playing poker real late and this girl started talking to me. She didn't have a uniform on but as it turned out she worked in the hotel ladies room. She was the attendant who handed out towels or whatever they do in women's restrooms. Beautiful girl . . . I got to know her and we started having an affair. Every night I'd gamble and have a few beers after my last show and then I'd go to my room and phone the hotel ladies room, "Well, I'm in my room now." A few minutes later there'd be a knock at the door and there she was. Bobby Hatfield and our bandleader Mike Patterson were running all over town looking for chicks and all I had to do was call the women's restroom—I always got a kick out of that. I'm not too proud of it now, but that was the life of a young performer in Vegas in the 1960s. The mob guys, Dean Martin, Sammy Davis, Jr., and Frank Sinatra—it was their world and we were just living in it.

One time Frank had to take a night off from the Sands to do a benefit in Los Angeles. He told Jack Entratter, "Put the kids in the big room tonight." He called us "the kids." What a thrill, moving into the main room even for one night, with the Count Basie Orchestra backing us (although they were not too happy about playing rock & roll stuff).

A few months later we got the call I'd been waiting for all my life. The Sands wanted to put us in the main room for an extended engagement. You have to remember, at that time Las Vegas represented the top of the show business world and the Sands was the top room there. Our bandleader Mike Patterson and I were like little kids, just thrilled. Mike went to tell Bobby the news.

Mike Patterson   I was so pumped and Bill was so happy. I drove to Bobby's house in Trousdale, I'd bought a dozen roses for his wife and my heart was going a hundred miles an hour. I said, "Bobby I'm so proud to be able to say these words to you. You'll

never guess what happened—we've been invited to
play in the main room at the Sands Hotel!"

"I'm not gonna do it, I don't want to do it," he said.

That broke my friggin' heart. I felt like asking
him what he was doing in show business. I mean,
he was the president of his high school class, he had
a contract to play pro baseball, and he could sing
like nobody had ever heard before—but he had no
dream. That's not a put-down, it was just the heart-
breaking truth about Bobby—he had no dream.

That's when it became crystal clear to me that Bobby and I were
just in two different comfort zones. It's not a right or wrong thing.
It's like a young married couple who grow older and one gains a
hundred pounds or one starts drinking or gambling. The other one
is like, "I didn't sign up for that." Bobby never signed up for #1
records and the main room in Vegas. He signed up for John's Black
Derby in Orange County.

When people lined up across the casino to get in to our lounge
show at the Sands, Bobby loved it. No sweat, a full house every show.
But the pressure of having to pack the main room and have our
name in huge letters on the Vegas Strip as headliners, that didn't
work for Bobby. He wasn't wired that way. As it was, he got so nervous before every show he'd throw up. We were just very different
guys, but thankfully, as you'll discover much later in the book, we
came to terms with that in later life.

After we'd conquered Vegas for rock & roll it was time to get
back in the studio and make another hit record. We did, but it came
out of left field and took us all by surprise.

11 | That's the B-Side?

Phil Spector had a strategy for leaving no doubt which side of a record should be played. In the 1960s all the radio stations got 45 rpm records (as did everyone else) with an "A" song on one side and a "B" cut on the other. Usually the B-side was a throwaway song but some artists, like the Beatles, actually had "2-sided" hits.

Phil was determined that would never happen with one of "his" records; he made sure the B-side was so bad nobody would ever consider playing it. For example, the B-side of "Lovin' Feelin'" was a horrible, I mean horrible song about a woman who plays piano in a bar called "There's a Woman." Don Randi, Phil, Bobby, and I went into the small studio at Gold Star Studios and wrote and recorded what may be one of the worst records ever. We were in and out in less than four hours; just goofing around and having fun. You can check it out on YouTube, type in "Righteous Brothers There's a Woman"—but lower your expectations. Believe it or not, some of the distributors called Phil and asked him what side to play. He said, "Are you fuckin' nuts? Play 'Lovin' Feelin'.'"

Phil's B-side strategy came back to bite him with our next release. We followed "Just Once in My Life" with "Hung on You." Unfortunately for Phil, but fortunately for us, the "bad B-side" Phil put on "Hung on You" was "Unchained Melody," which became a monster hit for the Righteous Brothers. That really pissed Phil off. First of all, regardless of what the label read, I produced "Unchained Melody," not Phil. The first 45s that were sent out listed me as the producer, but when it became a hit, suddenly the labels were changed and Phil's name was there as producer. I even played the Wurlitzer piano on the cut. Believe me, if I thought it was going to be a hit I'd have hired a real piano player.

Phil was livid, he started calling radio stations and telling them to stop playing "Unchained Melody." I can't fathom why Phil didn't hear what a great record that was. He was by no means an idiot. When it came to music he was brilliant. I don't know why he didn't hear that it was a hit, but he came to terms with it. He brought us all together, me, Bobby, and our agent Jerry Perenchio, to sell us his idea for the next song. It was not a happy meeting, not for me at least.

I assumed it would be another song from Barry Mann and Cynthia Weil, or Carole King, or one of the great writers from the Brill Building in New York, but that's not what Phil had in mind. Phil said, "The natural song would be 'Ebb Tide'." Both Roy Hamilton and Al Hibler had hits with "Unchained Melody" and "Ebb Tide" so there was a natural progression that made some sense.

At first it felt OK to me, then Phil said, "And, I think Bobby should do it by himself." You could almost hear the ripping apart of the Righteous Brothers. Remember, Bobby didn't know that Phil had tried to talk me into leaving him; now Phil was reversing course.

Jerry was adamantly against it, "Absolutely not, no!" Then he asked what I thought and I said, "Maybe, I don't know where it would fit, but apparently my voice is reasonably commercial and I could be on there somewhere." Phil stood his ground, "Nope, Bobby needs to do it all by himself." Phil was paying me back for turning down his offer to go with him solo and for producing a B-side that outperformed his A-side creation. Finally Phil asked Bobby what he thought and Bobby said, "Yeah, I think it should be me alone." Jerry and I got up and walked out.

Phil wasn't into "Ebb Tide," not at all. He wasn't even there when Bobby put his voice on the record. Really, on what Phil Spector production had Phil Spector ever given someone else any creative control? Bobby did a great job and the record did reasonably well. By the way, that really high note at the end of "Ebb Tide," Bobby put that in there as a joke and Phil kept it in the final master. I liked the recording, but I wasn't involved at all and that really was the start of Bobby and me pulling apart.

In some ways I thought, "Good for Bobby." He got his payback for his smaller roles on "Lovin' Feelin'" and "Just Once in My Life," but it strained our relationship. Our next record would help heal the wounds a bit. It was, in my opinion, a really good Righteous Brothers record because it was Bobby *and* Bill. It was certainly one of our biggest hits.

12 | Soul and Inspiration

In 1966, we were out of our Moonglow Records contract and had signed with MGM, so I called Barry Mann and asked what happened to that song we were working on in New York to follow "Lovin' Feelin'." He said they hadn't even finished it. I said, "Finish it."

Not only did he finish it but he brought me four or five other songs, including "We've Gotta Get Out of This Place," which was a giant hit for the Animals. I passed on all but "Soul and Inspiration." I produced "Soul and Inspiration" and there we were again, back on top with the #1 song in the country. In fact, "Soul and Inspiration" stayed at the top of the Billboard charts even longer than "Lovin' Feelin'." Back to the pressure and I was frazzled.

It was a very cool but very strange time for music. The hippies, long hair, and all the psychedelic stuff was coming in. Two huge producers approached me and said, "We'll give you a million dollars up front if you grow your hair long, grow a beard, and put together a rock band with horns." Blood, Sweat, and Tears and Chicago were

56

burning up the charts, and they thought I could do the same thing. I turned them down. Six months later I had long hair, a beard, and a horn band, but no million dollars!

It was also a very strange time for America. Racial tensions were reaching a breaking point and we felt like something of a bridge between the white and black music and the young generation of both races. After "Soul and Inspiration" we were asked to be the first-ever white headliners at the legendary Apollo Theater in New York. Everything was set, but then New York Mayor John Lindsay asked us to cancel the date. He was afraid there could have been violent protests, so we didn't do it.

Still, I wanted to go back to our R&B roots and keep moving forward and that was way beyond Bobby's comfort level. He was mentally still back at the Sands Hotel lounge doing "Little Latin Lupe Lu," that's where he felt at ease. His "camp" of friends and my camp started to clash. Somehow there was this vibe that because I hadn't graduated high school and Bobby had attended college he was the "brains" behind the Righteous Brothers.

His people were telling Bobby he was the cute one and he was the smart one and he shouldn't listen to me. I'd heard a couple of things people around Bobby had said; "Bill's a babbling idiot" was one comment that really pissed me off. I'd had it, I was hurt. As easy as it was to become a Righteous Brother it was just as easy for me to say, "Fuck it." With three million dollars on the table in bookings and guaranteed money I said, "Fuck it." I stayed for another six months because Jerry asked me to, but I told Bobby, "I'll stay for six months, but I'm not doing all these corny jokes, we're just gonna play it straight." For six months we did the show straight and I thought it was the best Righteous Brothers ever. I didn't do anything to look pissed off onstage but I was through. I had done everything I could to move Bobby out of his 1963 comfort zone and I got my lunch handed to me for it.

> **Bandleader Mike Patterson**   I had an epiphany.
> It wasn't until Bill and Bobby broke up and I stayed
> with Bill that I realized Bill was a genius. I know
> he won't be comfortable with me saying that but he
> really was. Bill put the shows together, he produced
> the records—he did everything. The arrangements,
> light cues—everything came from Bill. It was like
> he had a vision for the way things would work and
> always knew what he wanted.

All the hassles and the frantic schedule of having a #1 hit again nearly killed me, literally. I can't give you a great perspective on that time in my life without introducing you to my wife Karen, who helped me make it through. I'm going to get a bit ahead of myself in my story, but I want you to know how much her way-too-short life shaped mine.

13 | Sweet Karen

Karen O' Grady was one great chick. Her life, our life together, and her murder changed me forever. As tragic as the end of her life was, the beginning wasn't all that great either. Her family was a disaster. Her dad used to beat Karen and her siblings and ultimately abandoned them. Her sister couldn't cope and spent time in what we used to call an "insane asylum." Her brother went to prison for spanking a baby so hard it died. There was sexual abuse in the house . . . and on and on. Not what you think of as the model 1950s American home. She didn't have an easy path in life, but I came to love her as a beautiful girl, inside and out.

I first noticed her at First Presbyterian Church in Santa Ana. That's where my folks went—as I shared earlier, I'm from a very religious family. Karen went to Santa Ana High; she was a couple years younger than me and was dating a guy who went to my church, so I knew who she was.

When we went to play at the Rendezvous Ballroom to unveil "Little Latin Lupe Lu" there were about a thousand beautiful young girls there, and Karen O' Grady was right in the middle of this audience. I swear, her face just lit up. It was unbelievable; I couldn't take my eyes off of her. When we got offstage I met her, got her phone number, and we started dating. As I said, just a great lady, great chick—but there was one thing: She was nervous about dating a musician. (Kind of like I'd be if my daughter McKenna was dating one now!)

I told her, "This is the only thing I know how to do." Since I'd quit high school—singing, performing, and hopefully songwriting seemed like my best or maybe my only good options. And it really *was* what I wanted to be, a singer/songwriter.

Karen just couldn't get past it, so we broke up. I was really heartbroken. My breakup with Karen hadn't been nasty, we both agreed it wasn't going to work—but I was still hung up on her. I ran into Karen and told her she was right. I was going to "retire" from my music dream at age twenty-one. She was thrilled and I was in love; we got back together as a couple. I just had to finish out some dates at the Rendezvous.

Then Karen got pregnant, so we thought, "Hey, we'll just get married." We both wanted to get married anyway, so the pregnancy gave us a nudge. We were married right away and boom, our little world started to explode! "Little Latin Lupe Lu" became a hit, then "My Babe," then we went on tour with the Beatles—it was crazy. It was way too much for us to handle, and while I was on the Beatles tour Karen had the miscarriage I mentioned earlier in the book.

When I came home we talked things out. It was obvious my life was going to continue to get pretty frantic. Without the baby to hold us together we decided to get a divorce. We also decided to make love one more time and apparently I hit the bull's-eye. She got pregnant with Darrin; thank God. Our thinking was, "OK, hold it, we're not getting divorced—this is gonna be great." As it turned out, at least career-wise, things were great. From the moment she got pregnant to the time she gave birth, Bobby and I got hired as featured cast members on *Shindig* and we recorded and released "Lovin' Feelin'" and it went to #1. In just nine months we went from being "Lupe Lu" sizzling to being TV star and "Lovin' Feelin'" flaming.

Unfortunately, that meant that when I wasn't on the road I was in the studio producing Righteous Brothers records. We were living in Orange, California, and I was driving back and forth to the studio in Los Angeles nearly every night. Darrin was about one at the time and I was emotionally and physically exhausted. We were about to move closer to Los Angeles when I fell apart. I had what doctors used to call a "nervous breakdown" and was hospitalized. When you're starring on a national TV show and have the #1 record in the country everybody wants you, everybody needs you, and they need you *now*! I went to the hospital to have a minor ailment checked, and the doctor said, "You're not going anywhere." I was such a wreck that Karen had to tell them my name—I couldn't even get it out. The doctor told me I was, "like an orange that had been absolutely squeezed dry." The doc kept me in the hospital so I could get some rest; unfortunately the young "Candy-Striper" girls kept waking me up at 3 and 4 in the morning to get my autograph. When Karen found out she flipped out. She got them to send me home so I could really get some rest. She was great—she took such good care of me and Darrin, who was still just a little puppy at the time.

As I recovered we bought this bitchin' house in Hollywood for $75,000. Today it's worth millions I'm sure. It was a great house, and it made it much easier for me to commute to the studio. I'd get home at 2 or 3 o'clock in the morning and Karen would often get up and make me tacos or something—what a great wife and partner. But, after a couple years we realized we were always visiting Orange

County because that was where our friends were. We'd end up sleeping on somebody's couch and soon decided we'd had enough. When Darrin was three we moved back.

At this time, late 1967 and early 1968, things were falling apart with the Righteous Brothers. I wasn't going to have Darrin raised in an atmosphere where his dad was considered an idiot. We moved back to Orange County, and I firmly decided I was going to leave the Righteous Brothers.

To fill out the time I'd committed to stay with Bobby we went on the road with the Blossoms, who we'd met on the *Shindig* show. They opened for us. At the time they consisted of Fanita James, Jeannie King, and Darlene Love. While we were on the road Darlene and I started an affair, which was really weird because when we were on *Shindig* we never even looked at each other that way. The truth is, Karen and I got married for the wrong reason. Just having a child wasn't enough to hold us together. Finally, I decided to get a divorce because I thought I was in love with Darlene, and it wasn't fair to Karen. Darrin was about five when we got divorced.

Not long after, Karen started dating a tall, good-looking athlete from Hermosa Beach, Jerry Klass. Jerry was a basketball player who worked for the Harlem Globetrotters. He was a white guy who played for the Globetrotters' opponent team, the Washington Generals. Occasionally, Karen and I would do things together with Darrin, like go on short trips to Palm Springs. I felt like I was falling back in love with her and kind of wanted to put things back together, but she didn't. She said, "No, I'm in love with Jerry." They soon married and she moved to Hermosa Beach. They had a son they named Damien—he's a great kid. As it turned out though, Jerry was kind of a playboy and womanizer, he forgot to stop dating other chicks and Karen knew. Not a bad guy; he just didn't know how to be married, and Karen grew weary of his infidelity and filed for divorce. Through it all Karen and I tried to maintain a good co-parenting relationship for Darrin.

Fast-forward to January 29, 1976, I went to pick ten-year-old Darrin up at Karen's house. The next morning Darrin and I were going to drive up to Lake Arrowhead to look at a cabin I was thinking of buying with my childhood friend Johnny Mohler. It was very odd. Darrin put his stuff in the car, and as Karen started to walk away she turned, came back, and gave me a big hug and said, "I love you." I said, "I love you too."

She was my best friend, not just Darrin's mom, but really my best friend in the world. I left with Darrin and the next morning Karen hobbled to her car on her crutches (she had broken her leg trying to ride Darrin's skateboard) and dropped Damien off at the now infamous McMartin Pre-school. That was the school that shortly after made national news for allegations of ritual sexual abuse.

Everything seemed normal as she returned to her house through the back door she always left open. But this was the last time beautiful thirty-two-year-old Karen would ever walk through that, or any other door. Some guy was waiting in the house. He attempted to rape her and strangled her with her own bra. Her two closest girl-friends told me they had plans to go to breakfast with her that morning after she dropped Damien off. They saw her car pull in the driveway and figured she'd be ready to go in a minute. She never called so they decided they should call her. They'd seen a weird looking guy walking around the neighborhood the past couple days and wanted to tell her about that too. Why they didn't just call the police I'll never know. They called her and nobody answered, and they thought, "That's weird; we know she's home, maybe she's in the shower." One of them went over and walked in the back door and saw her crutches lying on the floor. She began calling "Karen, Karen," but there was no answer. As she got closer to the bedroom she just sensed something was wrong and panicked. She ran out of the house, got her friend, and they both went back to the side of the house and listened. They could hear what sounded like Karen whimpering but thought maybe it was the television. Then they went to the front hall and the same guy they'd seen lurking around the neighborhood for two days stepped out and said, "Hi girls," and then made his escape. They ran to find Karen on the floor and called the paramedics. She hadn't had any oxygen to her brain for fifteen minutes. Even though one of her friends was a nurse, there was little anyone could do . . . she was barely alive. The police have never solved the crime, and the case remains open to this day. Every few years it pops up again, like a kick in the gut.

That morning Darrin and I were on our way to Lake Arrowhead, and we'd stopped at a town called Blue Jay to see Jerry Klass' parents who lived there. Darrin went in the house to say hi to his step-grandparents and came running out saying, "Mom's been beat up!" I thought, "beat up?" So I went inside and they told me there was an attempted rape, but they didn't really know how bad it was. We hauled ass back to Hermosa and I went to the hospital and into the room where Karen was. God, I just hate to remember that moment because for years, when I think of her that's the face I see. I saw this beautiful young girl with this horrified look on her face, because it was the last minute of her life. I was pissed. I was scared. I was everything all at once. They told me to sit there and hold her hand and talk to her because they didn't know what she could hear and not hear or understand. It was the hardest thing in the world for me to do. I told her, "You're gonna be fine. We're gonna get through this. The kids are gonna be great. I love you. Thanks for being such a great mom." What do you say looking into that frozen terrified face? That look on her face; I will never forget it, ever.

I was a wreck. I called my manager David Cohen and my friend Johnny Mohler to come to the hospital and just hang with me, thank God they did.

David Cohen   It was a Friday during the day. I got the call from Bill, "Karen's been raped and she's dying." I quickly drove down and when I got to the hospital he was outside, and the two of us went in together. I looked at Karen through a glass window with Bill standing next to me. She was on life support and absolutely gone. He and I held each other and stood there crying for what seemed like quite a while. Then we went outside and sat in the camper truck that Johnny had come in. We spent a good part of the day and night in that camper. I wasn't even there fully mentally, it's still a blur.

I'd come to the hospital every day to talk to her and finally they closed her eyes and that made it a little easier. At one point I whispered in her ear, "If you wanna go, go. I'll take care of Darrin and if I need to I'll take care of Damien too—I'll be there for them." This was the time for me to keep a promise I'd made her long ago and not always kept, that I would be there when it was important for the family.

By that time we knew that if by any chance she lived she was gonna be a vegetable—but I was certainly more than willing to have her come live with me and Darrin, even in that state. One day I arrived at the hospital to find that, without my knowledge, they had taken her off life support. Because her divorce to Jerry wasn't final apparently he had the legal right to do that, but it really pissed me off. Not only did I have to deal with my feelings, but now I had to tell my 10-year-old son his mother was gone. He never got to say goodbye.

Darrin was inconsolable, with deep wailing sobs. "No. No, I need her!" I'm not sure where I got the words, but they just started coming out. I said, knowing he was attending Catholic school at the time, "Darrin, you believe in God, Jesus, and heaven right?" He said, "Yeah." I continued. "You understand about eternity, here we are for maybe 100 years and eternity is forever. When Mom was in that hospital she more than likely had a meeting with God and said, 'I don't want to leave my children.' And God probably said 'what's the big deal, they're gonna be up here for lunch.'" That seemed to make sense to him. Then I said, "Heaven is beautiful, more beautiful than we could possibly imagine. If you, me, and Mom were in this big mud pit and it's about thirty-feet deep and there's no way to the top, but somehow Mom figured a way to get up there—and it's beautiful up there, we wouldn't say 'no, no, no Mom—come back down to the mud pit.' We would be thrilled that she got up there because sooner or later we're gonna get up there too. We're not gonna ask her to come back down to the mud pit." He really got that.

I'll never forget the first Mother's Day after Karen passed. All the kids in school had to write a Mother's Day card for their moms. Darrin wrote me a Father's Day card. I can still see Darrin and his five-year-old little brother Damien standing in the bathroom at my beach house brushing their teeth getting ready for bed. These two beautiful little boys, it just broke my fuckin' heart. Like, "Oh shit, they lost their mother," that was the first time it became real to me. I was sad and very pissed at the same time; I wanted to find the son-of-a-bitch that killed their mom. Over 35 years later I'm still looking for him, I've got a private eye on the case. It's like a bad movie; it just stops my heart to talk about it. Thank God, Darrin turned his tragedy into triumph—he was a great boy and now a great man, I couldn't be more proud.

Karen would be so proud of him too. Both he and Damien are doing so well, great Christian men with great families. Darrin used to perform with me regularly, he's a terrific singer, and for years he was the lead singer for Paul Revere and the Raiders. Now he owns a successful cable TV business, and one of his star employees is his half-brother Damien.

Darrin Medley   I work as a volunteer in a trauma intervention program called TIP. Recently I had to console a family who'd just lost their mom and one of the kids cried out, "How am I gonna live without her?" That really struck a chord with me because that's exactly what I told my dad when mom died. When she was in the hospital in a coma I kind of knew it might happen; I was preparing for it to happen—but to hear him say, "She's gone" was pretty tough. He handled it really well, he always allowed me to express myself emotionally and feel my feelings.

I'd like to say I have closure at this point but it's funny, I've felt like I had closure five or six times. At the different stages of my life it comes back up. When I got married and had children the wound seemed to open. Every time it's taken me to the next level of my life.

I was ten and Damien was five when our mom passed. I kind of felt I had to step up and be the big brother. Damien and I are very different, he's very introverted and I'm the opposite. He deals with things by not talking about them, so I made sure I was actively involved in pursuing our relationship. Dad has always encouraged me to do that. Then when Damien's dad Jerry died in a car accident when he was twelve, I really wanted to make sure he was OK. When he graduated high school he came to live with us and our relationship has blossomed ever since. Today he's my best friend and the vice president of my cable TV company. We're very, very close.

Karen left a great legacy in Darrin and Damien and so many other lives she touched, but there aren't enough words to tell the legacy she left in me. I'd change everything to have her here, but the heavy cost of her passing made me be a man, maybe for the first time. I became a celebrity at age twenty-two. I was making huge money, had women throwing themselves at me—it became my world. I thought everything and everyone was playing by my rules. Thankfully, I got sucked back into the real world. After Karen died I had to decide if I was going to raise Bobby Hatfield or raise Darrin. That's how much energy it sucked out of me to maintain the working relationship with Bobby. It was no contest. The next thing I knew I was out on a school field trip with fifteen moms watching for whales off the coast. I wasn't a Righteous Brother, I was Darrin's dad. That was a real jolt, a real eye-opener, and it was the best thing that ever happened to me. It changed me. My life wasn't all about me anymore—it was about Darrin.

So, thank you Karen. You gave me more than I could ever repay. I did my best to raise Darrin the way you would have wanted me to; he's doing great. It's been an honor to be his dad and it was an honor to be your husband and have you for my best friend. As I've always said—you are one *great* chick.

14 | The "New" Righteous Brothers

Even though Bobby and I had agreed that neither of us would ever take the name "the Righteous Brothers" and use it with anyone else, that's just what Bobby did. In 1968 he teamed up with a great singer, Jimmy Walker, who'd been in the Knickerbockers and they were together for about four years. They worked, performed our old songs and even recorded some new ones, but it never took off at all. It just wasn't Bill and Bobby. That odd, weird tension we had worked for us.

I advised Bobby against it. I didn't feel it was right for him to make money on what we'd created together. He finally said he'd pay me a percentage for two years and then the name would come back to me. I never saw a dime. I always thought, and I told Bobby, "Man, you're one of the great doo-wop singers in the world. You should get two guys, a black guy and a white guy, and either one can do my parts, but just do that in your show. When you go record, do it alone and those guys can just back you up." He said, "No, I've already met with Jimmy and we've got it worked out."

Then I got an incredible call from Jerry Perenchio.

"Hello?"

"Bill, this is Jerry; how big are your balls?"

"Give me a minute to check."

"Seriously, Sarah Vaughn just dropped out at the Cocoanut Grove and they have an opening. I can put you in there solo for three weeks. How big are your balls?"

Now, at the time, the Cocoanut Grove was the hottest night club in Hollywood. I didn't have a band, I didn't have a show—I didn't have anything except Jerry's belief in me. I hired Dean Martin's comedy writer and a band with backup singers and put together a show. Everybody who was anybody in Hollywood was there opening night. It was unbelievable. Sammy Davis, Jr., was supposed to introduce me but at the last minute he had to drop out so they called in Bobby Darin.

After he introduced me he sat down in front with the Blossoms (including my then-girlfriend Darlene Love) and believe me, the Blossoms take no prisoners. They'd sung backup on nearly every hit record of the day, and they didn't tolerate bullshit. But, if you got it right and hit a note they liked they'd be on their feet shouting, "Sing it brother!" Pretty soon the whole crowd was doing it. I looked down and saw Bobby Darin jivin' and clapping, and I knew I was going to be OK. It was a thrill.

That's when I really started to grow as a performer and as a man. I quickly became "Bill Medley," not just half of the Righteous Brothers. It felt incredibly good. I started to become confident in who I was. One funny thing happened that I couldn't get my head around—my audiences were packed with women. Not the teenyboppers who first embraced the Righteous Brothers, but mature attractive women. I couldn't figure it out. I never felt like someone that women would swoon over, I didn't see myself that way and still don't. I asked my manager at the time, Jim West, what he thought was going on. He said, "Bill, I think they wanna get with you." I was really taken aback by that, it kind of shocked me. When I was a Righteous Brother I just took it for granted that the girls were screaming because Bobby Hatfield was the blond, cute guy.

Part of me was like, "That's bullshit, I'm a singer and I want them to come in to hear me sing." Now, was it a problem that gorgeous women like Mary Wilson from the Supremes were sitting down front? Not so much! But it really did surprise me that some women would see me that way. Bobby had always been the "spokesman" of the Righteous Brothers onstage. Some people clam up when they get nervous, but Bobby was the opposite. When he'd get nervous, which was about every moment onstage, he'd start talking and anything could come out of his mouth—anything. That would scare the shit out of me when we'd go on *The Tonight Show* or something like that because I never knew what Bobby was going to say. I always felt like the cop around him in public. When we broke up it was like a weight off my shoulders.

The tension that we had, me being the cop and Bobby the unpredictable loose cannon, kind of made us who we were. It was a lot like Dean Martin and Jerry Lewis, the differences in us made the act funnier. When I went out on my own I finally got to let a bit of my real self come out. Even the corny jokes my comedy writer came up with gave me something to talk about.

"I went on a diet and lost a partner."

"I just came from Vegas where they have all those topless shows. Hey, if you've seen one you've seen them both."

I quickly abandoned that, and as I started coming up with my own funny stuff, I began to like who I was. Like, "Wow—it wasn't just Bobby being cute and us having some hit records. People are actually interested in Bill Medley." It felt good.

I only saw Bobby and Jimmy perform as the "New" Righteous Brothers once. They were opening for Connie Stevens, who I was dating, and I went to see her. I thought they were really good but they just didn't have the same chemistry. Jimmy was the same height as Bobby and he had a great voice but very different from mine. The visual magic wasn't there; it just wasn't Bob and Bill—the tall skinny guy with the deep voice and the short cute guy with the high voice. It didn't work and not because of the lack of talent. It would be like Dean Martin trying to replace Jerry Lewis or vice versa. It just didn't work.

I decided to keep moving forward and my next stop was the recording studio, where Carole King brought me a new song with an incredibly ironic title for a guy who's just broken up with his partner.

15 | I Can't Make It Alone

Carole King's "I Can't Make It Alone" was the first song I released after Bobby and I broke up. Is that nuts or what? It was a great song and a good recording, but it did nothing on the charts. The next song did a lot better, it was Barry Mann and Cynthia Weil's song "Brown Eyed Woman."

I had rented a house in Hollywood and Barry asked if I had a piano there, which I did, so he came over. He said, "I've written a song but I need to explain it to you. Now listen, this has never been done, it's about a white guy in love with a black woman. He's saying, 'I love you' and she's saying, 'Stay away baby.' Are you willing to take that risk?"

As soon as he said that Darlene Love came walking out of the kitchen and Barry said, "I'll take that as a yes."

Barry Mann   When Cynthia (Weil) and I wrote the song we had no idea that Bill and Darlene were dating. When we played them the song Darlene actually thought we knew about it and had written the song especially for them. It was a hit in New York, LA, and Chicago, but they wouldn't play the record down south.

Talk about art mimicking life. When I recorded "Brown Eyed Woman" Darlene sang backup and was right there with me.

Darlene Love   What happened was that Bill was having a hard time getting the right mood as he was singing it. I was in the sound booth and they called me out into the studio and they dimmed the lights. I stood right in front of him while he sang the song. The feeling was unbelievable, to have someone record a song that's about you right in front of you. That's the first *and* last time that's ever happened to me! Actually, it was the first time a song like that had ever been written, especially in the rock & roll world. I mean, a white man and a black woman? C'mon, not in the 60s.

Barry Mann co-produced the record. We had six black girls singing background, all great singers. Darlene, Mary Clayton, the Blossoms, and Edna Wright—it was fantastic. Just hearing them rehearse with the piano changed my musical life and thinking about how I wanted to perform. I listened to the record just the other night and I can hear those girls like it was yesterday. It gives me chills. There's a humanity that comes out of Darlene's voice that is just so real—she's one of the best singers in the world. She's also one of the greatest people I know.

It's funny, for some reason I've always been able to stay close to women I've dated, even after we break up. As much as I'm sure I frustrated them with my "in and out," behavior, they were always kind. I think it's because I dated some great women. I've always said I come into relationships like a Rolls Royce and leave like a dump truck. For much of my life I just wasn't able to commit, although something must have changed because I've been married to Paula for over twenty-seven years. She may be the most patient woman alive, you'll meet her later.

I really have dated some of the greatest women in the world. I mentioned earlier that Mary Wilson and the Supremes used to come to my Vegas shows and sit down front. I'd go see them perform too. This was after Diana Ross had left the Supremes and Mary was leading the group and doing an incredible job. Because she was in the background when Diana was there a lot of people never knew what a great singer and performer Mary was—and still is. After a while Mary and I became more than friends and we had our "moment in time" which, true to my form, was kind of an on-again, off-again thing. Great lady—funny, talented, and so real.

About that time Connie Stevens came to Vegas to work in the main rooms. She was another talented singer and performer—she really put on a show. Because so many people knew her from the movies I think they were surprised to find out how good she actually was. She was dating songwriter Jimmy Webb at the time and I think that's how we connected. I'd traveled with Jimmy to Brazil to sing one of his songs at an international song festival.

She'd come into my show a lot and one night we ended up at the blackjack table together, laughing and having fun. I walked her to her room and even though nothing happened that night, it was the beginning of another on-again, off-again relationship that lasted years.

I'm sure it still pisses her off that I never would commit. Once she proposed to me, not necessarily to marry me, but maybe so we could get married and then she could leave me to get it out of her system.

Connie is one of the most spectacular women in the world. She puts her money and her time where her mouth is—going to Vietnam and the Persian Gulf War with Bob Hope to entertain troops or whatever. She's like the Energizer bunny; she just goes and goes to help people. When Karen was murdered, Connie asked me if she could raise Darrin. She said, "I'll do this for you." Darrin's probably pissed I didn't let her. To this day she and Darrin have a close, almost family-like connection. Connie and I had a really great relationship for the five or six years we were together as a couple. I was just one of those schmucks, scared to death of commitment.

Connie Stevens   I always kind of took to Bill, he was my kind of guy. I was appearing at the Landmark Hotel in Vegas and there was a large robbery. The robbers broke into my room with my infant children there; it was terrifying. Then my conductor went to get us some food and was killed crossing the street, I was a basket case. Bill Cosby came to my suite first, but had to leave, so the Righteous Brothers came, and I reacquainted with Bill then. Bill was very sympathetic and a good friend, but it was a lost time for me. With his ex-wife Karen being murdered we were kind of thrown together by the tragedies. His little boy Darrin just captured my heart; I always took to him like he was mine. We'd go on vacations and I just fell for the family. Later when Darrin

got hurt in a motorcycle accident I flew to the
hospital, it was like it was happening to my own
child. Maybe it was a little bit of my own ego and
my love for Bill, but as Darrin grew I felt that if
I wasn't around he'd be lost.

I was in love with Bill for years, but we were
always on and off. When we were in an "off" period
he met and married his second wife Suzi. I hadn't
heard from him in a long time and he called one
day out of the blue and said, "I won't be calling you,
I'm getting married."

I said, "Well, you haven't been calling me
anyway." That was typical of Bill Medley; he felt he
had some kind of obligation to let me know. Bill is
rock solid; he's a man's man, extremely talented
and so charismatic. He has way more than most
I've seen.

In the middle of my "in-and-out" times with these great ladies
I met another terrific woman and fell for her. "Woman" would be
a stretch—she was just nineteen. Suzi Robertson was a cute little
hostess at this restaurant called the Fiddlers Three. I was alone,
still on the rebound, and even though I thought she was too young
for me (I was thirty) I asked her out. Our first date was on a boat.
We were with Johnny Mohler, his girl, and some guys I didn't
know who owned the boat. I was scared to death when I went to
pick her up because her dad was a lifer Marine and I was this long-
haired rock & roll guy. It turned out he was a Righteous Brothers
fan and a great guy, but I didn't know that then. I said, "I'll have
her home early."

We left for Catalina Island but we got fogged in and couldn't get back. She had to call her Marine father from the ship-to-shore radio on the boat and tell him we couldn't get back. A nineteen-year-old girl and this thirty-year-old singer are stuck on the ocean on their first date and can't get home that night, yeah right. When morning came and the fog burned away we saw that we were in Laguna Beach, just off the shore. I took her home and apologized, and they were cool, but what they didn't know—and I didn't know either, was that the guys who owned the boat were drug smugglers. The whole time we'd been at sea the boat was packed with marijuana. They got busted two weeks later and that's how we found out. Wouldn't that have been a career stopper for me! Imagine the headline: "Righteous Brother Caught Smuggling Dope with Nineteen-Year-Old Girl!"

We kept dating for about six months and decided to get married. It was 1970 and I was starting an emotional oblivion season of my life. She was great, but I didn't really think it through. About six months into the marriage I knew that even though I loved her, it wasn't going to work. I was thirty and her life was just starting, I didn't want to drag her through five or six years of a bad marriage. The logic didn't work, and I'm a logical guy.

We went to my lawyer buddy Marvin Cooper and sat down in his office. He said, "How are we gonna do this?"

Suzi said, "What do you mean?"

"How are we gonna split this up," he said.

I was prepared to take a financial bath. I had just made my deal with A&M Records; I think they gave me half a million up front. I'd earned a lot of money in the short time we were married. Suzi said, "Listen, I didn't teach him how to sing. I don't want anything." She wouldn't take anything. Finally I talked her into letting me buy her a Porsche, but that was it.

"What are you giving this to me for?"

"Suzi, you walked away from a lot of money. You could have killed me—at least let me do this for you."

We got an annulment. How or why that worked I don't know. To this day she and her husband Scott are friends of mine. I recently had dinner with them in San Diego after I'd done a concert there. Another great lady in my life.

So, at this point I had one marriage and one annulment. I had another of each on the horizon. I dated Janice Gorham in Jr. High School and High School. Shortly after Karen passed away I reconnected with Janice, but I was out-to-lunch mentally. I went on-and-off with her in my typical Medley bullshit dance for years. Finally I asked her to marry me and told her I was ready to quit the business; I was fed up. Even though she'd been dating a handsome lawyer, Scott McEwen, she agreed to marry me. In hindsight, I think she wasn't really over Scott or at least confused about that. Again, about six months in we both knew it wasn't going to work. I came home from the road, she was very depressed and it was over. Another annulment. I haven't stayed in touch with Janice; I hope she's doing OK.

Now I'm up to one marriage and two annulments. Before I get to my next (and hopefully final) marriage I want to take you back to the music and possibly the performance highlight of my career.

16 | Hey Jude

March 12, 1969. The *Grammy Awards*, the music industry's biggest party, was being held at the Century Plaza Hotel in Los Angeles. I wasn't the hottest guy in the business at that point, I'd left the Righteous Brothers and just had one minor hit on my own, "Brown Eyed Woman," which was really only hot in New York, LA, and Chicago.

My agent called and said they wanted me to sing one of the five songs nominated for record of the year at the *Grammys*. It was quite a strong field—Simon and Garfunkel's "Mrs. Robinson," Bobby Goldsboro's "Honey," Glen Campbell's "Wichita Lineman," Jeannie C. Riley's "Harper Valley PTA," and the Beatles' "Hey Jude."

They gave me my choice and I said I'd do "Hey Jude." The producers said, "What, no, that song's all wrong for you." I told them I'd do that or nothing because I knew in my mind I could make it a Bill Medley song. They finally said, "OK, it's your call." All through my career I did what people told me I couldn't do, like being a white guy singing black music. I wasn't trying to be difficult, it just felt right.

I did the arrangement with Bill Baker, who did the arrangements for many of my hits, and started doing "Hey Jude" in my show so I could get comfortable with it. It went over great so I knew it would turn out fine at the awards. Mike Patterson came with me to the *Grammys* and we rehearsed the band in the afternoon. Lou Rawls, who was singing "Honey" as part of the show (talk about an odd pairing of artist and song) heard the rehearsal and called his manager. "You've got to be here at the show tonight, you're gonna see something remarkable," he said.

Bill Cosby was the host of the *Grammys* and introduced me and the nominated song. Mike Patterson began to play the piano intro, *dee-dee, dum-dum,* like a little vamp. I came out and my mic cord was caught under the stand. I didn't want to untangle it clumsily so I took my time and all the while, while Mike is playing the piano vamp, you could feel the energy starting to build. Then I started to sing, just me and the piano, *Hey Jude. . .*

Like ripples of a tidal wave the strings came in, then the band, and as I got to the bridge, *Anytime you feel the pain . . .* Glen Campbell, who was sitting in the front row, jumped to his feet and shouted, "Sing your ass off, Medley!" By the time we got to the *Na, na, na . . .* part the whole audience was on their feet singing along, and it got bigger and bigger. The horns were screaming and it was thunderous. Then I went into this "preaching thing," ad-libbing lyrics and the blacks in the audience started singing back at me answering what I was saying; it was magic. When I finished I got a long standing ovation from my peers, it felt incredible. I walked offstage and I remember standing in the wings exhausted, panting—like I'd given a two-hour show in just one song. Bill Cosby came over to me and said, "They won't stop applauding—go out and take another bow." I went back out and took a bow and they were just yelling. I walked offstage and it kept going. Cosby came to get me again, "Bill, get out there and take another bow." It literally stopped the show.

Gossip columnist Rona Barrett, who was the TMZ-type celebrity reporter of those days, was there and she wrote, *Bill Medley stopped the Grammys; he got a five minute standing ovation.* It was a great moment for me. I don't tell the story much because it sounds like I'm bragging, but it was unreal, like an out-of-body experience. The only time I've ever come close to that feeling was when I was singing at Darlene Love's father's church. Her dad was a pastor and we were at a service and he said, "Let's get Bill up to sing." I sang "Precious Lord." I was singing to the Lord and the whole church was right there with me. I had always sung for the audiences, but this was different, I felt I was singing right to God.

Darlene Love   I don't know if Bill was going to church much at that time. When I told my parents I was dating Bill they asked me to bring him to church. When we (the Blossoms) were working with Elvis, "Precious Lord" was one of the songs he loved to sing. Bill was there with us after the shows, banging out the old-time Gospel standards, songs that everybody in that world knows. Now, Gospel piano players can just about play anything—tell them the key or just start singing and they follow you and that's what happened in my dad's church. When Bill started singing it was just him worshiping God, I think it was a new feeling for him.

After the *Grammys* my phone started ringing off the hook. Everybody in the business called my manager David Cohen. Fortunately for me, my record contract with MGM was just ending, so the timing was perfect. Herb Alpert, the co-founder of A&M Records, made me a great offer. They gave me some big front money, and Herb said they'd do whatever I wanted—any producer or whatever. Herb is one of the nicest guys in the business, just a wonderful man and humanitarian. The minute I signed the contract Herb took me in the back room and said, "I want to produce you." That made me a little nervous because I wasn't sure if we'd be a good combination. Herb was brilliant with the Tijuana Brass and so many others, but I didn't know if it would work. He said, "Let's just find great songs and have as little background as possible." Far different from the "wall of sound" days I'd had with Phil Spector.

We started going through songs and I found a Carole King song I wanted to do. Herb called Carole and she came in and played piano with just an upright bass. It sounded like a hit record to me but Herb said, "No, I don't think so." The song was "You've Got a Friend." I really believe it would have been a hit just as it was with maybe a flute or some other minor additions. Well, we know now what a hit it was for James Taylor—just another in a long line of songs I didn't do that ended up being hits for others.

I think I've turned down nine careers worth of hits. Among my brilliant decisions, here are a few of the songs I passed on:

- Elvis' "In the Ghetto"
- Eric Burdon & the Animals' "We've Gotta Get Out of This Place"
- Paul Revere & the Raiders' "Kicks"
- The Hollies' "He Ain't Heavy, He's My Brother"
- Gladys Knight's "Neither One of Us Want to Be the First to Say Goodbye"

Oh well, that's show biz.

As it turned out, Herb and I had very different visions for what the next Bill Medley record should be. Herb brought in my friend, the great songwriter Paul Williams, to write lyrics for French composer Michel Colombier. Michel's new album was called *Wings*—it was a Blood, Sweat and Tears kind of thing with a symphony orchestra playing jazz and fusion. Herb asked me to sing a couple songs on the album and I said, "Sure, I'll do it," but it was way over my head. I'm a twelve-bar blues singer from Orange County, and it just wasn't me. I could hardly find where "one" was. I felt like a junior high jerk and I finally had to tell Herb, "Just point at me when I'm supposed to come in." They'd already recorded the tracks and they were literally about two notes too high for me, I had to sing some of it in falsetto. It was fun to do and I learned a lot, but I knew it wasn't going to do anything on the charts. One of the songs I sang did get nominated for a Grammy, but it had no commercial appeal.

Still, off my *Grammy Awards* "Hey Jude" performance I was getting hot again, so back to Vegas I went. That's when I really became close with Elvis.

17 | Elvis

Since Elvis passed away a lot of people have claimed to be his close friend, some have even written books about it. I can tell you that Elvis really didn't have many close friends. He wouldn't, or maybe couldn't, let people inside his world. His manager, Colonel Parker, and his Memphis guys protected him from everybody who wanted a piece of his time and talent. For some reason though, he let me in. In private life he was not the guy the public knew, he was actually shy and insecure, a lot like I was—maybe that's why we connected.

> **George Klein** As far as real friends Elvis had five. Actors Nick Adams and Jack Lord, Sammy Davis, Jr., Tom Jones, and Bill Medley—that's it. You might add Ann Margaret to that list, he'd made *Viva Las Vegas* with her, but as guy friends go he just had those five guys. We were all Righteous Brothers fans and for some reason Elvis just loved Medley. They got real close when they worked

together in Vegas. Maybe it's because Bill is so real,
no bullshit—he tells it like it is.

My friendship with Elvis really began to take shape in 1968. I was recording on my own in Memphis with legendary record producer Chips Moman. Chips also produced many of Elvis' big hits, including "In the Ghetto" (which, as I said earlier, I stupidly turned down), "Suspicious Minds," and "Kentucky Rain." I'd record during the day and Elvis would send one of his guys over to bring me to Graceland at night.

Everything you've likely heard about Graceland living during Elvis' glory days is probably true and then some! There was always something fun going on and Elvis always had his guys, his bodyguards or "The Memphis Mafia" as they were known, to cater to his every need and laugh loudly at his every joke. Joe Esposito was kind of like the leader of the Memphis crew, Elvis really depended on him to handle things. For the most part I found them to be basically good guys who were along for the ride. I mean there was always plenty of good-natured mischief, food, money, and women to go around.

One of my great memories of Graceland is the night Elvis decided we were going to the movies so, naturally, he had to rent out a theater to avoid the throngs of fans. As we walked out of the mansion to Elvis's limo he opened the rear door and in his halting, country-boy accent mumbled something like, "Bill, ah, ah, I, I, I. . ." and he motioned for me to get in the back of the limo. Then he and Priscilla got in the front seat and Elvis drove toward the gate. In those days, at any given time there were 200 or more people gathered at the Graceland entrance, hoping to catch a glimpse of the "King." As the gate slowly opened the fans began to shriek, and as the limo passed through not one single person looked in the front seat! All eyes were fixed on the back where I was. I just smiled and waived at 200 of the most disappointed Elvis fans in history.

About this time, toward the end of his movie career, Elvis was kind of like the Howard Hughes of rock & roll. Outside of those of us who got inside the walls of Graceland few people ever saw him in public. One night when I was performing solo at the Sands in Las Vegas there was, however, an Elvis sighting to remember. Now, this was 1968 and Elvis was at the height of his fame. I had a little comedic Elvis "bit" in my show where I talked about our friendship, mimicked his awkward speech patterns, and said I never understood what he was saying, all in good-natured fun. The crowd always ate it up, as they did anything Elvis. One night, about ten minutes after doing my Elvis shtick, the house maître d', who had to be about eighty years old, shuffled up to the stage to hand me a note. The note simply read, "He's here." I read the note out loud to the crowd and said, "Who's here?" Then I jokingly said, "Oh, I suppose Elvis Presley is here?" Just then in the back of the room a guy stands up and starts singing "All Shook Up." It was Elvis! The house lights came on and the crowd went bananas. It took me about twenty minutes just to get them back.

Elvis returned to live performing in 1969 at the International Hotel in Las Vegas. He had a pretty good run there, over a seven-year period he did 837 consecutive sold-out performances to more than 2.5 million people. Fortunately for me (and I've always thought Elvis had something to do with this) when he was there, I was there performing in their 600-seat lounge. When the curtain went down on his shows a recording of his voice would urge concertgoers to "go over to the lounge where my friend Bill Medley is performing."

The International is where I really got to know Elvis the person, not just the star. His first show was at eight o'clock, mine was at ten o'clock. His second show was at midnight and mine was at two o'clock in the morning. When he was getting ready for his second show he'd often call my dressing room and ask me to come be with him while he got ready. Then he'd usually send his bodyguards up to take their positions and it would just be me, Elvis, and his hairdresser alone. We talked about anything and everything and I could see there was a deep insecurity and vulnerability underneath the shell of the world's most manly man. We probably had fifty or more of these quiet chats and I really got to feel comfortable talking with him—just two guys shootin' the breeze. One night he asked me to come to the stage and watch him go on from the wings. So, we're waiting and the band starts that "2001 Space Odyssey Theme" that was his trademark entrance song. The women started screaming and the emotion and energy level of the room went nuts. His backstage handlers started to fix up his collar and hair with final touches so I backed away a little bit, about ten feet. When I saw him standing in the shadows with all that power about to explode I thought, "Holy crimony, that's Elvis Presley!" I had gotten so comfortable with him as my talking buddy I'd forgotten he was probably the biggest star in the world at that time. I got so excited I wanted to run onstage myself!

As our relationship grew some really funny things happened. One night I was doing my 10 o'clock show and Elvis was walking through the backstage kitchen area. He heard me singing the Righteous Brothers hit "Lovin' Feelin'," which he also did in his show. He turned to his bodyguards and said, "Hey man, Bill's doin' mah song." Next I noticed something stirring on my left as Elvis walked onto the stage followed by his four bodyguards. He slapped me on the shoulder and said a friendly, "Hey Bill" and they just kept on walking off to the other side of the stage. To say the place went wild would be an understatement. Now, in those days Vegas was a small town. By my two o'clock show it was all over that Elvis had walked onto my show and there were long lines outside the lounge in hopes that he would do it again. I'm thinking, "Yeah, right—like he's gonna walk through again!" So, the show starts as usual and, again, I'm in the middle of "Lovin' Feelin'," right at the emotional peak—*Baby, baby I get down on my knees for you*—and here he comes again. Only this time he's followed by eight of his Memphis guys and ten hotel security guards. They simply walk across the stage and every one of them pats me on the shoulder and says, "Hey Bill." Of course the place went nuts. It was what the crowd had hoped to see but didn't really expect.

Finally after I finished the song I just stood there and took a long pause, almost Jack Benny-like, and said, "OK, I don't know who he is, but now he's startin' to piss me off!" That had to be the best punchline of my career—the crowd howled! He heard I said that and actually called me to make sure I wasn't really angry. I said, "Are you kidding, my next show's at eight o'clock, could you be there please?"

In some way, maybe to hide some of the sadness or pressure he felt, Elvis was almost always joking around. One night I was sitting in the front row at his show and he was about to sing "Lovin' Feelin'." He knew right where I was seated and he always started that song with his back to the audience, his legs spread out in kind of a karate stance. The band would start and he'd spin around to face the audience as he sang the first line, *You never close your eyes anymore. . . .* With his back to the audience he snuck a peek at me and whispered off mic, "Eat your heart out Medley." At the same time, with his hand placed on the back of his thigh he proceeded to stick out his middle finger and give me "the bird." I sometimes wonder how many people saw that and what they thought if they did.

Elvis was big on inside humor while at the same time very sensitive to others' feelings. For example, he always introduced me to the crowd when I attended his shows. One night he forgot. Backstage after the concert in his dressing room there was the usual background noise buzz from his Memphis guys and the associated hanger-on crowd. As I got up to leave Elvis stopped me and said, "Hey Bill, sorry I didn't introduce you tonight." I said, "It's OK, but I'll never come back again." The room fell silent and Elvis looked at me with a hurt little boy face. I mean he was really wounded. Seeing this I instantly said, "I'm kidding!" The tension was cut and things returned to normal. As I shared, down deep Elvis was a very sensitive and fragile guy.

What happened to Elvis in the following years is one of my saddest memories. I knew he'd been using pills for a long time, in fact he offered me some once. We were in his room and he opened a suitcase with this huge stash of all different kinds of pills. I declined but he assured me, "Bill, I really know what I'm doing." I suppose all addicts feel they have a handle on their struggle. One time when he was admitted to Baptist Memorial Hospital in Memphis for addiction treatment I tried to get in to see him. I can't say who the gatekeeper was for sure, but they wouldn't let me through. It was so hush-hush they didn't want word to get out.

Another time, toward the end of his life, Connie Stevens and I went to his hotel room. "Let's get him out," she said and we convinced him to leave the room and come to dinner. At the last minute he chickened out, it was really sad to see what was happening.

Connie Stevens   We were all appearing in Vegas at the same time. Bill and I were going together and I had dated Elvis for a time too. I told Bill, "Elvis is

locked up in his room, let's go steal him. We can go
out for pizza and hang out." Bill said, "Yeah, let's do
it!" We went over to the Hilton and called and talked
to Elvis' guy Joe Esposito. He said, "Oh my God, that's
great, come up the freight elevator." We snuck into
his room and Elvis was really happy to see us, he said,
"Ah, now this is a good thing, a really good thing."
We said, "Come on, we came to steal you" and he
said, "Great!" We waited around, the place was just
jammed packed with people. Then Elvis disappeared
into a room. When he came out and looked at us we
both knew he wasn't going to go. He was a different
person. He was gone. I'll never forget that moment;
it was not long after that he passed away.

The very last time I saw Elvis was when I took my son Darrin
backstage to meet him. We didn't find him in his dressing room; he
was sitting in the hotel stairwell talking with one of his backup
singers. He was wrecked, hardly coherent. I didn't want to embarrass
him, I quickly introduced him to Darrin and we said our goodbyes.
As I walked away he turned to me and said, "Bill, it's going to be
alright man." It wasn't. August 16, 1977, Elvis passed into eternity at
age forty-two. Ultimately, he gave way too much of his life away to
make other people's lives work. Elvis Presley was a good guy, and he
was my friend.

Seven years after Elvis passed I found myself still thinking about
him a lot. Every time I'd hear one of his songs I remembered the
good times and the bad, I couldn't get it out of my system. I wrote
and recorded a song called "Old Friend." It was kind of like my love
letter to him, things I'd say if I had the chance. It went like this . . .

Don't Be Cruel, Teddy Bear, dancing hips, and long black hair—old friend, you crossed my mind today. Las Vegas hotel, Graceland, sweet young daughter, and a million fans—old friend, you touched my heart today. If I listen to you close in the still of the night, I can hear your voice saying you're alright. Close my eyes, open my soul, touch the King of rock and roll—old friend, it's good to feel you once again.

You shook us all up, you loved us tender. Caught us in a trap, we all surrendered, uh huh, oh yeah, loving you. Don't. Baby treat me nice, I'm falling in love with you. I can sit down, put your records on, seven sad years are suddenly gone. God you were young, it doesn't seem fair. Would you be here if I could've been there? Old friend, my heart's crying once again.

Trapped here on earth, your mother was free. A lonely pain we refused to see—old friend, you touched my heart today. Old friend, I'm missing you once again.

18 | No Voice, No Choice

As I shared earlier in the book, Vegas can be tough on a singer's throat. Especially a guy like me who likes to let it all hang out, shouting from deep in my soul. I was still doing great business, but even the crowds began to see I was struggling. Really, what was I going to do if I couldn't sing? I certainly couldn't go back to Bartmore Beauty College and pick up my hairdresser career.

It started in about 1972. I was still recording for A&M and I could tell that I wasn't hittin' it—I wasn't able to do exactly what I wanted to do. I'd been doing three shows a night at the Hilton, and my throat got bad, and then I was singing on top of it. It's like running on a sprained ankle—It ain't gonna get better; it's only gonna get worse. It got worse and worse. I went to my throat doctor, Dr. Barton, one of the big throat guys in Beverly Hills, and he said, "Bill, I'm sorry. I think you need to quit singing. Don't sing anymore, your throat's just hamburger meat."

Well, I didn't want to hear that, so I went to see Dr. Kanter, who was *the* vocal chord guy in Hollywood. They'd just started filming vocal chords at the time and he filmed the inside of my throat and said, "Yeah, you need to retire. Your vocal chords are gone."

They were. I can remember standing on the stage with sold-out audiences and I was so depressed. The curtain would be down, and I could hear the people talking and the excitement in the room, and I remember looking at the band and thinking, "I don't even know how I'm gonna get the note out." As a singer I still had the notes bangin' around in my head—I knew where I wanted to go but just couldn't get there. It was humiliating.

A lot of celebrities and other singers used to come see my shows, and I noticed that they started dwindling away. One of the singers told me, "We just know that you're going through a real tough time with your throat, and it's kinda painful to watch because we care about you."

I can't begin to tell you the depression and frustration I felt. I went out to the Balboa Pier in Orange County, near my house. I might have had a few beers in me, which I usually did. I was out at the end of the pier, crying and sobbing, yelling at God, "Why do this to me? Why did you give this to me to take it away? Why did you do that?" I was pissed at God. "Please, please; you gotta help me!"

Two weeks later I was somewhere, I don't even remember where, and I bumped into Jack Coleman, who was my high school choir teacher and a very religious man—a good Christian. Thank God for guys like Jack and others in my life who are great Christians, because I know so many self-righteous "pretend to be" Christians that aren't. If they were all I had to see, it wouldn't scare the hell out of me, it would scare the heaven out of me!

Jack was this beautiful man who really took me under his wing when I was in the high school choir. He knew I was a troubled kid, but he also knew I loved music, and he knew I was a good singer. He was in this great Gospel quartet, and he'd take me to Los Angeles to watch them record at Capitol Records. A lot of people say, "Boy, if it wasn't for this one teacher who paid attention to me . . ."; Jack was that guy for me.

So, all these years later I run into him, and he asks, "How you doin' Bill?"

I replied, "I'm done. I can't sing anymore, and I'm done."

Now, at that time Jack had retired from teaching and was giving voice lessons and leading a church choir. He said, "I can fix that for you."

I told him, "I've been told by the two biggest throat guys in the business that I'm done."

He said again, "I can fix that." He was giving voice lessons for $15 a shot, and he probably needed the money.

So I started with two lessons a day, five days a week. An interesting thing happened in my head. Before I lost my voice, I was very certain that I was lazy, that I'd gotten lucky with the Righteous Brothers thing, and that I was stupid. I was convinced of that, and Bobby was very supportive of that thinking. That's how I went into all of this—two lessons a day, five days a week. And I could hardly even whisper the vocal exercises he had me doing. Jack would say, "OK, do it again."

After about three months of this, I realized that no one had paid him. I said, "Jack, I'm so sorry. Give me your information and I'll have my manager get you a check right away." I felt really bad about it.

Jack said, "No."

"Really, Jack. Just write down your information and I'll pay you."

"No. About a week before I ran into you, God told me to heal you."

"What?" I'd never told him about the pier thing or anything like that.

He said, "God has His hands on you, and He wants me to heal your voice."

He wouldn't take any money—he never did. He was, however, taking his church choir to Europe and I got to donate some money for the trip. That's the only way he'd let me pay him.

Jack Coleman got me my voice back. I promise you, he was the only man in the world I would have sat there and done those "la-la-la" voice exercises with. I'm just not that patient. I'm not gonna work that hard at anything. God sent me, literally, the only man I would have done that with.

Through all that I found out I wasn't lazy, and I found out I wasn't stupid. It was like God said, "You think you're lucky? You think you're lazy or don't care? Watch this." Whoop! He took it right out and made me go to Him, and He showed me how bad I wanted it. That's my opinion and nobody can convince me otherwise.

Sometime later we used Jack's choir for a big outdoor concert at the Greek Theater in Hollywood. Bobby got to know Jack a little bit then, and after we rehearsed, something incredible came out of Bobby Hatfield's mouth. I'll never forget it.

He said, "Now I know what God's like."

I was stunned. Stunned! He wasn't joking, he didn't have a one-liner after it, just "Now I know what God's like." Jack Coleman got my voice back, but if he were here, he'd tell you he was just doing what God told him to do.

19 | The Second Time Around

In the early 1970s the Sands decided to convert its lounge into extra gaming space, so Mike Patterson made a great deal for me over at the Las Vegas Hilton, which used to be called the International. We had a killer band and I did three shows a night there for the next few years. It was a time in my life when I really *needed* to work. I was still in and out of relationships with this girl and that girl, trying to nurse my voice back to health while making a living.

There were two girls who really caught my attention during those years—beautiful, funny, and sweet women. They may be the only two girls I never got the courage to ask out. The first was Lola Falana. She's been out of the limelight for many years now, but in the late 1970s Lola was called "The Queen of Las Vegas." She played to sold-out crowds at the Sands, the Riviera, and the MGM, and then the Aladdin offered her $100,000 a week to headline.

Lola was a great performer, singing and dancing like crazy, just gorgeous. For about a month straight she'd come to my shows and then back to my dressing room after. I really liked her—she was a down-home, funny chick. We became good friends, and I always thought that maybe she wanted me to make a move, but for some reason I was afraid to ask her out. She was a lot of woman.

David Cohen teases me about it still because Lola Falana was his dream woman. Our mutual friend Quincy Jones once arranged for Lola to sit next to David at the *Academy Awards*. He was in heaven. I just never got the nerve to ask her out. I'm pretty sure she would have accepted. She used to call me "Sweet Thunder." I was still wrestling with getting my voice back and I'd complain about it to her and she'd say, "Bill, honey—you're voice sounds like sweet thunder." I loved that name so much that I titled my next album *Sweet Thunder.* Nobody knew, until now I guess, why I did that.

I lost contact with her after a while and heard she had some severe health problems with multiple sclerosis. I think she's living in Las Vegas and doing better now. Someone told me she spends a lot of time working with a ministry that helps orphans in Africa. Good for her. Every time I'm in Vegas I think, "I wish I knew where she lived, I'd love to say hi." Maybe someone will read this and tell her. It would be great to catch up.

The other girl who really got my attention during those years was Goldie Hawn. She'd work the main room while I was in the lounge and she'd come in to my show. I had known her a bit from the 1960s and, like Lola, we started hanging out in the dressing room after. I think she wanted me to ask her out, but I was afraid. I was in awe of her; she was one of the cutest, funniest girls I'd ever met.

I never got the courage to ask her out, and right after she left there she started dating Bill Hudson of the Hudson Brothers. They eventually got married and there was a funny headline about it in the paper. It read, "Goldie Hawn Is Marrying Bill Medley of the Righteous Brothers." They were close; she married a "Bill" and he was part of a "Brothers" act. I could fill a book with all the wrong things that have been printed about me over the years.

I've never seen her since, but I had such a crush on her—I don't think she ever knew. I'm so happy for her though, her kids are doing so well and she eventually got with Kurt Russell, who seems to be a great guy. I don't know him, but I think he's the kind of guy I'd want to go have a beer with. It feels like they really landed on their feet.

Even though I was starting to get my voice back, it was still a strain, having to carry the whole show three times a night. In 1974 I asked David Cohen to negotiate an extension of my contract at the Hilton.

David Cohen   I was in town one day to see Bill and came away with the thought that he was just killing himself, because his voice was really struggling. He was singing very hard and doing three shows a night. He asked me to come in to see what I could do to make a new deal with the Hilton, so I sat down with the top guy and made a stud-horse deal for three years for big numbers. On my way up to Bill's suite to tell him I was thinking, "This is gonna be really hard because it hurts me to see him struggling so much onstage." I felt I had to bite the bullet and be honest with Bill; I've always been straight with him.

I went into his suite and said, "Bill, I've got you the deal of a lifetime here, it's just amazing—but I'm going to recommend you don't take it."

"What are you talkin' about?" he said.

I told him, "This is the hardest thing I've ever done, but I'm going to recommend that you go back with Bobby—if you don't, you'll have no voice left."

He looked at me and said, "Yeah, I hear what you're saying. Ugh, I think you're right."

We turned the deal down and set out to find Bobby.

I appreciated what David did; he cared enough about me to tell me the truth. I thought, "I'll just go make a couple of million dollars and retire." I made that decision based on sound, logical advice from David. It was the first time in my life I'd ever done anything purely for money and I discovered that the "make a pile and retire" motivation didn't work for me. If I had a decade I could erase from my life it would be the 1970s. And, even though it was the right thing to do for my voice, I actually lost money by becoming a Righteous Brother again. In the end, reuniting with Bobby became a good thing—but we didn't start on the best note.

David and I were shocked when we found Bobby. Bobby was broke and living alone in a small apartment in Costa Mesa, which he was going to be evicted from in a week. He wouldn't have been homeless, I'm sure his family would have taken him in, but he was in a bad place. He had a chair, a black-and-white TV, and a bed—that's it. He looked like a bum; we just gasped.

Bobby's sister-in-law Jeannie once said, "Bobby just has a lucky horseshoe up his ass." I guess that's true because a few days before he was going to be thrown out of his apartment I knocked on the door and said, "Let's go be Righteous Brothers again." I loaned Bobby thirty-five grand, we got him into an apartment, he got a much-needed facelift, and we started working again. Bobby didn't even rehearse, I rehearsed the band and Bobby just showed up and did the songs. It was just like when we were making records. I'd produce the records, lay down all the tracks, and then Bobby would show up with a case of beer and sing his part. That was Bobby's idea of working, he had such natural talent he could do that.

After David Cohen got us back together he began to put out feelers for a new record contract. He met with Haven Records, which was being distributed by Capitol, and they made a deal. Then we began looking for the right song and producer. At that point several people were interested in producing us, including Stevie Wonder (who we'd known since he was "little" Stevie Wonder) and Barry Manilow. As great as they were, neither of them felt like the right fit.

We met with Dennis Lambert and Brian Potter, who'd been writing and producing for the Four Tops and the Grass Roots. A couple years later they produced our old friend Glen Campbell's "Rhinestone Cowboy," talk about a range of musical styles. They brought us a song written by Alan O'Day and Johnny Stevenson that had first been recorded by the band Climax in 1972. It didn't do much for them but with some updated lyrics and the Lambert/Potter production, it sure did something for us.

Within a few weeks, a few *weeks* mind you, we recorded "Rock and Roll Heaven," and it became a monster hit. Not as big as "Lovin' Feelin'" or "Soul and Inspiration," but on July 27, 1974, it peaked at #3 on the *Billboard* charts behind John Denver's "Annie's Song" and Elton John's "Don't Let the Sun Go Down on Me."

We never really liked the song because it didn't have the old Righteous Brothers feel, but a hit record is a hit record. Everybody thought it would be just like the old days, so Jerry Perenchio booked a tour of 20,000-seat venues and off we went. Jerry must have lost his ass, because every single one of those dates had about 2,000 people showing up. It just wasn't the same.

Still, "Rock and Roll Heaven" kept us working steady through 1976, when my first wife Karen was murdered. As I shared earlier, after that my world was just a blur and I had to decide whether I was going to raise my ten-year-old son Darrin or my thirty-six-year-old partner. When I told Bobby I needed to take time off to raise Darrin he was pissed. I wasn't leaving the group; I just needed to be at home and Bobby didn't get it. He was so angry that he wrote me a horrible letter. I meant to save it, hoping that some day we'd be able to talk about it when things had calmed down, but I eventually threw it away. He really chewed me out for going off and leaving him behind. I *wasn't* leaving Bobby behind; I just took time off to raise Darrin. I quit performing my solo act too; it wasn't about Bobby, the act, or me—it was about Darrin.

Bobby didn't see it that way; he couldn't understand that Darrin was more important to me than him. I think he felt I left him out there to drown; he felt abandoned. I thought it was a no-brainer that I'd go off to raise my ten-year-old son after his mom had been murdered. Like, "Bobby, you're not my responsibility, I'm not even leaving you, I'm still your partner—I'm just taking some time off."

The reality was Darrin couldn't raise himself, he was ten years old! Bobby could have always gone out and made a living—for crying out loud, he was a Righteous Brother. I never discussed the letter with him because when we weren't working we never saw each other. We hardly ever talked, we never confronted each other, and we didn't hang around together; we weren't that kind of friends.

Since Bobby passed away I've thought a lot about our relationship. What dawned on me last year is that I'm really angry at him, because he didn't allow us to be good friends, to have the warm friendship we should have had, that we could have had. He didn't allow me to love him, and I did love him—he just didn't let me do it. It really pisses me off now, because I want to look back on the Righteous Brothers as this great, wonderful thing and this great, wonderful relationship with Bobby. He just wouldn't allow that to happen. I'm not sure he allowed it to happen with anybody.

When people say, "You and Bobby must have hated each other!" I think, "Are you kidding?" Hate is just not in my DNA. I hate things, like prejudice and other stuff, but I do not hate anybody. I didn't always *like* the way Bobby acted—but I *loved* who he was down deep inside.

Sometimes I think his connection with me was even worse because I was the guy who could make him rise to the occasion, and he hated that. It pissed Bobby off to have to rise to any occasion like, "C'mon, we have to rehearse," or go meet some other obligation. He liked to go on the road, because it was like a big "boys club" where you leave your family at home and have fun, but he didn't care much for the work. That made our relationship really tough because he knew how much work I was doing and how much he wasn't. He was scared people were gonna think I was more important, or that he didn't matter. Bobby was very insecure, almost like a scared little ten-year-old boy, even when he passed away.

Before "Lovin' Feelin'" we had our regional hits "Little Latin Lupe Lu," "My Babe," and "Koko Joe." That time was just fun rock & roll stuff, and our relationship was very good, because we were just takin' it as it came. We went from making a hundred dollars a week to maybe a thousand dollars a night! We thought we'd died and gone to heaven.

As I've said, we were just two twenty-three-year-old nutballs, like Butch Cassidy and the Sundance Kid with women, money, and booze. Sometimes we were half-drunk onstage. I don't know that we didn't care; we just didn't feel it was gonna last. Remember, I was a street guy, and Bobby was kind of this preppy college kid. All of a sudden he was becoming a rock & roll guy and he started living that life.

We had a great time, and we were unbelievable onstage. I listen to that old stuff now and I think, "No wonder!" We were just plain good, and we were crazy onstage. We'd get down on our knees and throw the microphone back and forth—performing like two black guys, making faces and sweating. We kind of gave that right to a lot of other white artists, to be emotional like that.

After "Lovin' Feelin'," the Righteous Brothers could have branched out into a lot of different areas. We could have been so much better, so much bigger than we were—but that just wasn't Bobby's comfort level. I think back to when we got together in 1962 as the Paramours. I'd be up there playing bass and singing and Bobby would just be sitting there. I'd say, "Bobby, come up and sing," and he'd respond, "Nah, c'mon—nobody's here, I don't wanna."

After the night was over, I'd say, "Listen Bobby, we're all splitting the money equally, you gotta pull your weight." When I'd confront Bobby like that he'd back down. He wasn't really a combative person; he just didn't have the best people skills. Bobby was one of these guys who would speak really harshly to someone, "Hey, where'd you get that shirt, that's a stupid-looking shirt."

"What?"

He'd say "I'm just kidding" but he wasn't. He was always as serious as a heart attack; he probably thought your shirt looked stupid. Still, if you challenged him he'd back off; in fact we never had an argument in our entire relationship. Seriously, never. He just wouldn't engage.

Bobby's mom was this sweet Swedish lady and his dad—well, Bobby grew up to be his dad. His dad was a little rough around the edges. It's just my opinion, but I've always thought Bobby was like his mom emotionally but to protect himself he took on his dad's persona.

Once I'd had enough. I told our manager David Cohen I was leaving the group. David stepped in and Bobby asked, "Why doesn't Bill understand that I'm just kidding?" David replied, "Because you can't rip somebody apart verbally and then say 'I'm just kidding!'"

Then Bobby told David something that really opened my eyes. "Every night at home we'd all sit there at dinner and my dad would make my mom cry, every night. We all thought what he was saying was funny, but she never got his humor." When David told me it dawned on me that Bobby and the other kids were laughing along so they wouldn't be next. He was a frightened little kid until the day he died.

Throughout the 1970s, while raising Darrin and growing up a lot myself, I began to understand Bobby. I didn't like a lot of things he did or said, but understanding him helped open the door for a much better relationship in our last twenty-five years together.

I can say this about Bobby; he was one of the great practical jokers of all time. Once we were playing in El Paso, Texas, just across the border from Juarez, Mexico. Bobby crossed over to Juarez and bought a huge stuffed iguana. It looked as real as could be. Somehow he got into my hotel room when I wasn't there and put it in the corner. When I came back from the show I turned the light on and walked right into it. I screamed and jumped about three feet in the air—I could hear Bobby laughing all the way down the hall. Another time he had a big lobster for dinner and, again, somehow got into my room and meticulously reassembled the lobster under the covers of my bed. When I flipped back the covers I freaked out. Of course, he came running over laughing his head off.

Bobby was also known for sending out great Christmas cards. One year he had a picture of him from behind with an open overcoat facing a fireplace, like he was "flashing" the fire. The caption read, *Chestnuts Roasting on an Open Fire.* Another year he sent out a picture of him and Elvis with the caption, *The King—and Elvis!* At the time I'm not sure if the practical jokes helped or hurt our relationship, but looking back now they seem pretty darn funny and creative.

My life has always been about relationships . . . with Bobby, my friends from junior high, my wives, kids, girlfriends—and so many others. Because of my social anxiety I've always moved toward those I felt safe with, and I ran from everyone else. Beyond my close circle, some of whom you've already met, I've been blessed to connect with a lot of great people. They've helped make me who I am today—let me introduce you to a few of them.

20 | Relationships

One of the benefits of getting famous is that you get to meet a ton of people. For me, that was also one of the drawbacks. I've never been comfortable around people I don't know. I have no tolerance for bullshit, and when you become successful everybody wants to be your friend. That's why I still hang out with the guys who knew me back in school, like Johnny Mohler, Ronny May, Steve Brooks, and Gary Stephens. They like me for *who* I am, not *what* I am. I've found some of those same genuine relationships in show business.

KENNY ROGERS

Kenny became a real good friend of mine back in the 1960s. Somewhere in the mid-1970s Glen Campbell invited me to a dinner with Kenny and David Gates from the group Bread. We sat down and had a few drinks and Kenny started telling us he was broke. He said, "Bill, I don't know what I'm gonna do." I went with Kenny over to his house and he said, "Thank God Marianne (Kenny's wife) is on *Hee Haw* because if she didn't have that work I'd be done. It's so bad that I'm going to old Las Vegas to the Golden Nugget." Kenny had monster hits in the 1960s with the First Edition and that shitty little lounge at the Golden Nugget felt like the last stop on the train. He asked, "Would you go work it with me? You'd be doing me a huge favor and you can use my band, they're great." They were great; Kenny still uses the same guys today. So, I did it. Steve Wynn owned the Golden Nugget in those days; he was just getting started on his rise to being a Vegas mogul.

Kenny told me, "Things are so strange in my career that I'm actually recording in Nashville." In those days Nashville was reserved for country music only, and country hadn't become big like it is today. I said, "What?" There was a huge separation between country and pop music back then, no crossover stars like we saw later.

I've always loved country music, I started to do a country album in 1968 when I left Bobby, but was told that wouldn't be good for my career. I ended up doing a country album years later and had a top 20 country hit, but at that time it was just weird. I tried to encourage Kenny, "That's cool, I think that's great. They've got good writers and producers there."

Fast-forward a few months to January of 1977—right in the middle of the disco music explosion. Kenny released "Lucille." Talk about playing against the trend, here's this pot-bellied, gray-haired guy singing, *You picked a fine time to leave me Lucille.*

The radio stations jumped on it and I called him. "Kenny, I think you've got a hit there." He said, "No, I don't think so, but I've got a couple other things coming out that are kinda Eagle-ish (the Eagles were just taking off) that will do better."

I said, "I'll bet you a thousand dollars 'Lucille' is a hit."

"Well, I'm not gonna bet against myself, but that's not gonna be a hit," he answered.

Boy was he wrong. "Lucille" was a smash. All of a sudden Kenny and that song were the hottest things around. Kenny called me and said, "Bill, my producer Larry Butler would love to produce you." I said, "I'd love to do a country album but I don't think so. I'm raising Darrin and I'm thinking I'll just ride off into the sunset with what's going on."

Kenny persisted, "C'mon, at least take a meeting with Larry Butler," so I did. I flew into Nashville. That day Larry was recording Johnny Cash. Larry invited me to the session and I met Johnny and went into the control booth. Almost bigger than life, Johnny Cash started laying down the vocal for the track, *You've got to know when to hold 'em, know when to fold 'em.* It was "The Gambler."

I thought, "What a great song," but I didn't think any more about it. Six months later Kenny released "The Gambler" and, again, straight to the top of the charts. I'm not sure why Johnny Cash didn't release it first. If Kenny was huge after "Lucille," he was huge on steroids after "The Gambler."

About that time I was really cash poor. I owned a restaurant called Medley's, which was tanking (more about that later) and I wasn't working much because I had to stay home with Darrin. I called Kenny. "I hate to do this, I've never borrowed money from anybody in my life, ever. You can have my publishing or anything else you want but I need twenty grand."

Without skipping a breath Kenny said, "Do you want to come up here and get it or do you want me to bring it down to you?"

"Wait a minute, I'm talking about twenty grand here," I said.

"Bill, come on up, I'll write you a check." Just like that. "I don't want your publishing or anything else, we're friends. Would you give it to me if I needed it?"

"Absolutely," I said.

"OK, absolutely, I'm giving you twenty grand."

I told him, "Kenny, it's a loan—I'll have it back to you in three weeks."

In a couple of weeks I put together ten grand and I walked into the studio he was working at. He was recording "Lady," Lionel Ritchie was there producing. That's when I first met Lionel. It turned out he was a big fan of the Righteous Brothers and I was a fan of the Commodores too. I gave Kenny an envelope with the ten grand. Kenny looked at me and asked, "What's this?" I said, "You loaned me twenty grand, and here's the first ten."

Kenny said, "No I didn't. I *gave* you twenty grand. Take this back."

"Kenny, this is your money. I borrowed it—this is yours!"

He said, "I refuse to take it. Do you know what's going on with me? Do you know how much money I'm making?"

He didn't mean that in an arrogant way at all. It was like he was saying, "Let me share this blessing." I dropped the envelope on the floor and said, "You can do whatever the hell you want to with it." He gave me a big hug, and I watched him lay down the vocal track for "Lady." A couple weeks later I got him the other ten grand back; I wouldn't have had it any other way.

A short time later I met Kenny's accountant at a party. He said, "Bill, of all the people Kenny's given money to you're the only person who ever paid him back. You've got a friend for life there." Of course, I had a friend for life in Kenny anyway; the guy didn't even want me to pay him back. That's Kenny.

Once he called me at Medley's and said, "Bill, I want you to see this house I bought." Kenny loved to buy and redecorate houses; he could have been an architect. He'd pay like twelve million for a house and then gut it and start from scratch. I've told him, "If I paid twelve million for something that fuckin' thing better be done!"

Anyway, Kenny said, "I'm here with Lionel (Ritchie) and you know he's a huge fan of yours. We're sitting here playing songs and I know you're a songwriter; I want you to come up." This is like ten o'clock at night, and I'm in Orange County and he's in Los Angeles.

"What?"

"Yeah, come on up."

I said, "OK," and I called my future wife Paula and asked if she'd come with me. We drove to Kenny's house and sat around taking turns playing our original songs. I've never really considered myself a writer, especially since working with people like Barry Mann, Cynthia Weil, and Carole King. But Kenny said something that night that stuck with me. He said, "I'm not a writer, but I know how to write." I thought about it. It's like, even though I've produced some of the biggest songs ever, I'm not a producer—I just know how to do it. Phil Spector was a producer. I was just a guy who learned how to do it.

So, we sat there at Kenny's piano trading original songs back and forth. Paula was loving it and so was I.

Paula Medley Bill didn't even tell me Lionel
was going to be there until we were driving up.
I was a huge fan of his and I especially loved Kenny.
We sat in the living room and all they did was keep
pushing each other off the piano bench, "Move over,
let me play you this one." I'm sitting there in an easy
chair three feet away watching this; it was kind
of surreal.

I was singing one of my songs and they decided they wanted to produce me. Right about the same time I'd heard from Barry Gibb of the Bee Gees, who were on fire at the time, saying he wanted to produce me. Wow, now what do I do? Let's see, Kenny and Lionel or Barry Gibb? Then I got a call from Richard Perry, who was producing the Pointers Sisters, Barbara Streisand, Neil Diamond, Donna Summer, and so many others—he wanted to produce me too!

How in the heck did I get three of the hottest guys in the business wanting to produce me at the same time? It blew my mind. I finally went with Richard Perry because he owned his own record company, but I was really honored that Kenny, Lionel, and Barry had interest. My relationship with and love for Kenny continues to this day. He's the real deal—talent *and* character, a rare combination in this business.

As I started to work with Richard Perry the strangest, almost surreal thing happened. It involved actress Kim Basinger. She doesn't know about it, I've never told this story before.

KIM BASINGER

This is going to sound like I'm crazy, but it's the absolute truth. In the middle of my divorce from Janice I saw Kim Basinger in some movie, way before she was famous. I just fell in love with her, what guy wouldn't?

Now, here's where you're going to start thinking, "Medley, you're nuts," and I probably was. From the mid-1970s to the mid-1980s I was waiting for the guys in the white coats to come take me away and lock me up.

To get over my angst and heartbreak with Janice I would go to bed imagining I was dating Kim Basinger. Sometimes I imagined we were married, I had a whole relationship with Kim Basinger going on in my head. The funny part is—it worked! When you're in love that's all you think about and it kept my mind occupied and helped me get to sleep. Again, I know what you're thinking—nuts.

This was the time when I was in the studio doing an album with Richard Perry producing. The one thing that bothered me was that he didn't pay attention when I was singing the vocal track. He was always on the phone ordering wine or something for fuckin' dinner while I was singing my brains out. Then when I was done he'd flip on the communication mic, "That's great Bill, can you give me another?"

I was right in the middle of a song and I looked over to the engineer booth to see if he was paying attention—and there's Kim Basinger! Just four feet away from me behind the glass she's watching me sing. I had just daydreamed about her the night before. I *literally* thought I was going crazy. Like, "Now you did it Medley, you're actually starting to see her." She was smiling at me, enthralled with what I was doing. I was in shock, thinking, "I might as well leave the studio right now and go straight to the Mayo Clinic or somewhere like that. Fit me up for the straightjacket, I'm done."

I walked into the booth, still not sure if she was even real. You can imagine my relief when she actually spoke to me. It turned out she was real and she was a Righteous Brothers fan. I'm still not exactly sure why she was there, I'm just glad she really was there. Whew, dodged the insanity bullet, but not by much.

I've never seen her again. I hope if she reads this she doesn't take it the wrong way. There was nothing ugly or sexual about my daydreams, I just mentally put her in my life to push out my frustration over breaking up with Janice. The fact that she happened to show up at my recording session during that time is beyond weird to me.

WAYLON JENNINGS

I was working in a huge showroom in Scottsdale, Arizona. I can't remember the exact year, maybe the late 1960s, long before anybody had ever heard of Waylon Jennings. I was kickin' ass, doing big business with huge crowds.

They had a great country bar downstairs and I've always liked country music—the real, old-time, shit-stompin' country stuff. Maybe it's because my dad's a Texan and the country boy finally came out in me, who knows? I'd go down there every night after my show and have them put a few beers on ice on my table and I'd watch the band. They just killed me; they were great. The singer would come over and we'd talk. It was really fun for me.

Just after that I signed with A&M Records, and I was in Herb Alpert's office one day and in walks Waylon Jennings. Herb said, "Do you know Waylon Jennings?" I said, "No, I don't. I'm a big fan, nice to meet you" and I shook his hand.

Waylon said, "Bill, it's me."

"What do you mean, 'me'?"

He said, "Scottsdale. We hung out for a month—we drank beer together every night."

I said, "You're not the country singer in that band are you?"

He laughed, "Yes!"

We became really good friends. When I was doing my country album in the 1980s in Nashville, Waylon and Johnny Cash came in to where I was having dinner and sat down with me. Maybe he had a few beers or something in him, but he sat there and just stared at me. Finally he said, "Yep, you're a fuckin' legend."

I said, "I'm a legend? You're the legend!"

If you look up the term "country music outlaw" you'll find a picture of Waylon. He wasn't too popular with the Nashville establishment in those days; he just did things the way he wanted to. I ended up being friends with most of the "outlaw" crowd. I met Willie Nelson through Kenny Rogers; I knew Johnny

Cash; and Kris Kristofferson became a friend as well, I did one of his songs.

I think what "outlaw" really meant was that they didn't follow the rules of Nashville. Of course, their substance abuse problems and bad behavior didn't help much either. They were just real guys.

Not recognizing Waylon and the story I'm about to tell you has changed the way I greet people. I never say, "Nice to meet you" anymore. It's always, "Great to see you." When I'm used to seeing people in one setting and then meet them in another I've sometimes embarrassed them, and myself. That's what I did to a pretty, dark-haired girl on the A&M lot.

THE DARK-HAIRED BEAUTY

I was on the A&M lot recording Kris Kristofferson's song "Help Me Make It Through the Night." He came up and introduced himself, "I'm Kris Kristofferson. You just recorded one of my songs, and I'm a big fan." I said, "Right back at ya, I'm a huge Kris Kristofferson fan."

About three days later I was still on the lot and this beautiful girl came up to me and said, "You're Bill Medley, aren't you?"

"Yeah."

"I met you in Memphis," she said.

I'm thinking, "Crap, did she have one of my babies or something?"

She said, "I met you in a nightclub and I told you I wanted to become a singer and asked what you thought I should do. You said to move to Hollywood and find a big act that you can be a background singer with. You said that would put me in the circle and one thing would lead to another. I did it. I moved to Hollywood and started singing background for Joe Cocker. After a while I got signed and I've done pretty well."

My dad Arnol, mom Irma, big brother Leon, and sister Barbara.

My junior high protector Billy Shiffer uses me as a barbell.

1st Presbyterian choir, in the front row, second from the left.

My class at Bartmore Beauty College. I'm seated down front with a goatee.

THE PARAMOURS   Personal Manager
                                 NAT GOODMAN
              Smash Records   HO 2-1115

The Paramours before
Bobby Hatfield joined—
Mike Rider, Sal Fasulo,
me, and Don Fiduccia.

John Wimber (playing sax)
put Bobby and me together
at the Black Derby.
He went on to start
over 1,000 churches
around the world.

****
THE HOT PARAMOURS
T.C.'s BLACK DERBY
****

THE RIGHTEOUS BROTHERS   Exclusive Recording Artists For   MOONGLOW RECORDS
Hollywood, California

Our very first promo photo as The Righteous Brothers.

Beach movies were hot in the 60s and we were California guys so we fit right in.

We had no idea why these new guys from England wanted us on their first American tour.

With Karen and little Darrin. I still get sick when I think about her murder.

Bill Medley Bobby Hatfield

THE RIGHTEOUS BROTHERS **exclusively on** **MGM RECORDS** R-1249

When MGM Records signed us away from
Moonglow our agent, Jerry Perenchio, got
us a million-dollar signing bonus.

The Righteous Brothers were the first rock act ever to play Vegas, but we had to get Frank Sinatra's approval first.

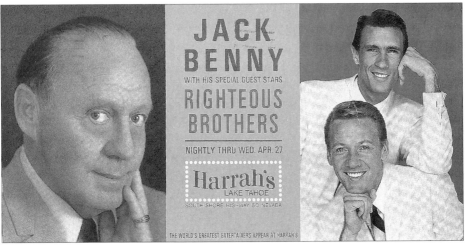

It was a thrill for Bobby and me to work with Jack Benny. What a great learning experience.

Ray Charles has always been one of my musical heroes. Once I had to sing *Georgia* with him seated just four feet away.

Growing a beard and long hair to test for the role of Jesus in the movie *Jesus Christ Superstar* caused some in the press to say I'd turned into a "hippie."

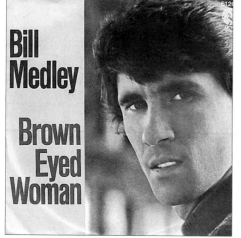

Barry Mann and Cynthia Weil's *Brown Eyed Woman* was my first hit as a solo artist, although most of the country wasn't ready for its interracial message.

FEBRUARY 13 THRU 26

BILL MEDLEY

FORMERLY OF THE RIGHTEOUS BROTHERS

FRANKIE ORTEGA & HIS ORCH.

AT THE AMBASSADOR HOTEL'S WORLD FAMOUS

COCOANUT GR🌴VE

GILBERT PAOLI, MAITRE D' & MGR. RESERVATIONS 387-7011

My first gig after leaving The Righteous Brothers was at LA's hottest club, The Cocoanut Grove.

It's been an incredible 28 years with Paula.

McKenna's first time on stage at Caesars Palace, during the *Dirty Dancing* tour.

Little "Mac" has grown into a wonderful and talented young lady.

I couldn't be more proud of Darrin. He's so smart and talented, but above all he's got a big, loving heart.

Singing with Jack Coleman's Ambassadors Chorale. Jack saved my voice, maybe my life.

Every time I go on stage it's like a first date. The audience is my date and I want to give them everything I've got.

When Jennifer Warnes and I recorded *Time of My Life* we had no idea it would become a monster hit.

Performing at the White House for the President and First Lady was a great honor.

Having Billy Joel induct us into The Rock and Roll Hall of Fame made it an extra special evening. I'm so glad we got in before Bobby passed away.

Paul Shaffer did an incredible job with *Lovin' Feelin'* at our Hall of Fame induction.

From a relationship standpoint,
my last years with Bobby
were my best years.

I said, "Geez, that's so great!" She gave me a big hug. I started to walk away and then turned back and said, "Excuse me, what's your name?"

"I'm Rita Coolidge."

I felt so bad. She was on top of the pop world at that time with a couple of hits and she was Kris Kristofferson's wife. I told her, "I'm so sorry I didn't recognize you."

She said, "Are you kidding? My God—you started my career. I did exactly what you told me to do and it happened just like you said it would."

What a gracious lady. But, from that point forward it was "great to see you"—not "nice to meet you."

KEITH RICHARDS AND THE ROLLING STONES

As I wrote about earlier, we did the Beatles' first American tour right before we got our national TV spot on *Shindig*. After that the Rolling Stones were coming over for about fifteen concerts in California, and they asked that we be on the tour with them.

Again, we were baffled. Why would they ask us to be on their tour? How do they even know who we are? Like the Beatles, they were part of that English "garage band" scene that loved the Righteous Brothers.

It was a great tour. They weren't really huge yet. And, like the Beatles, they were just really good, down-home guys. It was a lot of fun and we got to know them very well. This was all before "Lovin' Feelin'." We just had our minor hits then.

When we did "Lovin' Feelin'" and went over to England to promote it, the Rolling Stones were so sweet; they came and met us at the airport! The press was just a mob because of them, not because of us. Hardly anybody in England even knew who we were.

The next day we couldn't even walk down the street in London. Our picture was in every paper. We must have done nearly seventy interviews while we were there—it was nuts.

I went to see the Stones a few years ago in Nebraska. A friend of mine is really close with them, and Keith told him, "Hey, bring Bill out here, we'd love to see Bill. Don't have him come to New York, Vegas, or LA because we're just swamped with all of what that is, a lot of 'stars' and such."

So as a surprise my friend bought us tickets to go to Nebraska and we went to see the Stones. The big country group Brooks and Dunn was the opening act. I was watching them from backstage and Keith sent one of his guys out to get me to come back to their dressing room. I opened the door and there we all were—Ronny Wood, Charlie Watts, Keith.

We talked for about an hour. Through all those years of not seeing Keith, it was like nothing had changed—he was just a good street guy. "Bill, how are you, so good to see you, so sorry to hear about Bobby, it was so much fun when we were on tour together. . . ."

We were telling old war stories when their longtime sax player Bobby Keys came in and said, "The band that's onstage has seven guitars!"

The Stones guys asked, "Well, how can that be, who is it?"

Bobby answered, "It's Brooks and Dunn."

Every one of them said, almost in unison, "Well, who's that?"

This was at a time when Brooks and Dunn were on fire, probably the hottest country act around—none of the Rolling Stones had any idea who they were. I guess living life as a Rolling Stone for almost fifty years kind of insulates you from the outside world.

I can say this, even though the years have put a few miles on all of us, to me they were the same guys I met in June of 1964 on their first American tour. Great band; great show; just great guys.

WHOOPI GOLDBERG

In 1992 Whoopi Goldberg was filming *Sister Act*, one of her most successful movies, in Reno. I was working there at the time and she came to see the show. She came backstage after and told me, "I'm a huge Bill Medley fan."

I said, "Well, you were probably a Righteous Brothers fan, right?"

"No, I'm a Bill Medley fan," she said.

Then she told me the story. When Bobby and I first reunited we did a big concert at Central Park in New York. There were over 200,000 people there. After the show the cops were trying to move us through the crowded backstage area and there was this little black girl pushing toward the front. She shouted, "Bill, Bill—would you sign this?"

I was so touched that this little black girl wanted my autograph that I stopped and signed her paper. Whoopi told me, "That was me—and I still have it."

Wow. That blew my mind because I was a huge Whoopi Goldberg fan too. A really funny thing happened that first night she came to see my show. I hadn't met her yet, but everybody in the place knew she was there sitting in the back of the room.

At that time, and I won't use his name, there was a really hot white singer burning up the charts who was being labeled as the next "blue-eyed soul" guy. He had a raspy voice and sang with a lot of emotion, he was great. To keep me, and maybe Whoopi, from getting sued—let's just say his name is "Joe Blow."

So, the show is on and I'm doing my Ray Charles segment. It's a medley of his great hits and kind of tells a story as it goes along.

It almost always goes over well but that night I was on fire; the crowd was eating it up. As I finished, just as the applause started to die down this unmistakable voice, that could only be Whoopi, screams from her booth in the back of the room, "Fuck Joe Blow!" The whole audience fell out laughing, so did I. I could hardly pull it together to finish the show. Since then Whoopi has become a good friend. She's a wonderful and talented lady.

SYLVESTER STALLONE

While my record "Brown Eyed Woman" only had modest success nationwide, it was #1 in New York and, apparently, one of Sylvester Stallone's favorite songs. So much so that in the original *Rocky* movie he sings part of it as he's running away from Adrian.

After his *Rocky* success he wrote and directed a movie called *Paradise Alley*. It was a story about three brothers that ends with a big wrestling match. The movie didn't do well at the box office, at least compared to his other hits, but the theme song was great. It was called "Too Close to Paradise," written by Carole Bayer Sager, Bruce Roberts, and Bill Conti—who'd done the original *Rocky* theme.

When they brought the song to Sylvester they asked who he thought should sing it. He said, "I'm gonna sing it, and I'm gonna do it just like Bill Medley."

I think they kind of bit their tongues and wondered how they could talk him out of it. They called me up that day and snuck me into the studio at midnight to learn and record the song. The next day they played it for Sylvester and he said, "I love it, but I'm gonna do it. Now I know how to do it."

He wrote me a real sweet letter after that, thanking me for coming up in the middle of the night, and saying he hoped I didn't mind that he took some of the vocal things I'd done and used them on the record.

A couple years later I got a phone call from Judi Barlowe Fields, my manager at the time. She'd gotten a call from Stallone's people saying they wanted me to be in *Rocky III*, the one with Mr. T. They wanted me to sing the National Anthem before the climactic fight at the end. The phone call had woken me up—and I'm not good in the mornings.

Judi Barlowe Fields I know better than to call Bill before two in the afternoon, but this news just couldn't wait. I called him at about ten in the morning and he answered the phone coughing and gagging for about twenty seconds and pushed out a, "Hello."

"It's me," I said.

"This better be good," he replied.

Through a hail of throat clearing I said excitedly, "Wake up! You're not gonna believe it but I just got a call from Stallone's office—they want you to sing the National Anthem in the next *Rocky!*"

Silence. Then, "Is that the one that goes, 'Oh say can you see' or 'O beautiful for spacious skies'?"

I was on the floor laughing, that's Bill Medley's humor. I spoke to him two or three times a day for all the years I managed him and every single day I laughed. That was my experience with Bill, I believed in him as an artist and it was always joyous.

By that time Sylvester and I had become friends. I sang at his wedding reception when he married the gorgeous model and actress

Brigitte Nielsen. Of course I said I'd do the song for *Rocky III*. I recorded it in advance and went to the set to film it. They had like five or six thousand extras in this huge arena and I was standing there as Rocky came in and then Mr. T. The crowd was cheering and booing and when they got in the ring they started fighting before the bell. I didn't even realize they were filming, I thought they were really pissed at each other and going at it. Then they filmed me singing the National Anthem, but eventually it was cut from the movie and I understand why. I agreed with the decision. I told them right as I was leaving the set, "I don't know if this is gonna work because it's so anti-climactic after that brawl before the fight. The song just stops the momentum."

That wasn't the last time I'd work with Sylvester though. I got a call in 1986 asking if I wanted to do a duet with Gladys Knight for the theme song of his new movie *Cobra*. I said, "Of course I would—who wouldn't?" I mean, Gladys Knight, she's one of the great singers in the world. The song was "Loving on Borrowed Time." It was a good song and a terrific commercial record. Very 1980s, but very good. Unfortunately, the movie flew right into the mountain and took the song with it.

Then a couple years later I was asked to do one of my favorite songs, "He Ain't Heavy—He's My Brother" for the *Rambo III* sound-track. Again, that movie didn't do that well—sometimes I wonder if Stallone thinks of me as the "kiss of death." I told him, jokingly, "Quit calling me! The guy who should be calling me is (the late) Patrick Swayze. I was lucky for him with *Dirty Dancing* and *Ghost*."

One funny side note about that song from *Rambo III*. The original hit with "He Ain't Heavy—He's My Brother" was with the Hollies, what a great record. As I mentioned earlier, it was one of the songs I'd stupidly turned down back in the day. When I got the chance to record it for this movie I was thrilled, I thought it turned out really well. Just a few months ago I did a tour in Brazil and when I was taking my final bow the audience started chanting, "Brother, brother, brother . . ." I didn't know what they were talking about. My bandleader Tim Lee said, "I think they want you to sing 'He Ain't Heavy—He's My Brother.'" I'm thinking, "How in the heck would these people know I recorded that song?" So, I sang the first line, "The road is long, with many a winding turn." They erupted into thunderous applause. *Rambo III* may not have been a big hit in the United States, but apparently it was in Brazil. I sang it a capella and the band learned it for the next show. How fun and crazy is that?

It's also been fun watching Sylvester succeed. His brother Frank became a friend too, he used to come down to my restaurant, Medley's, and we'd hang out. Good guys, real guys.

JOHNNY CARSON

In the late 1960s, Lake Tahoe had beautiful lounges in their casinos; it was a great place to work. I was at the Juniper Lounge at the Sahara and Johnny Carson was playing in the main room. One night at my 3 a.m. show there's maybe nine drunks in the audience; it was just dead. I told Lee Ferrell, my bandleader, "Listen, just have the band play for twenty minutes and I'll come up and sing three or four songs and we're done."

I went to the bar and was having a beer; mentally I was done for the night. The bartender said, "Bill, does it make you nervous that Johnny Carson's in the room?"

"What?"

He said, "Johnny Carson's sitting right there."

I looked over and there he was, with a beautiful lady. I thought, "Oh my God!" I ran backstage and tried to get Lee Farrell's attention so I could come out and perform. I did, but I felt torn about what to do. Do I introduce Carson and maybe embarrass him because of the small crowd, or do I leave him alone and risk pissing him off, like, "What an asshole, he didn't even acknowledge I was there."

Finally, I thought, "Screw it, I'm gonna introduce him." I began a long, glowing tribute, because I loved the guy. Right as I said his name one of the drunks stood to get up and go to the restroom. The light guy thought it was Johnny Carson and put the spotlight on the drunk guy going to take a leak. The guy started waving as the people began to applaud. Carson is standing in the middle of the room, in the dark, laughing his ass off. Thank God he was a great sport about it. I always wanted to tell that story on the *Tonight Show* afterwards, but never got the chance.

BOBBY DARIN AND NINO TEMPO

Bobby Darin was a fantastic talent. Singer, songwriter, actor—he could do it all. His live shows in Vegas were unbelievable, packed with energy, even though his heart condition sometimes caused him to leave the stage for oxygen. You could never tell by the way he performed, he was great.

Nino Tempo became a friend of mine in 1963 when he and his sister April Stevens had their #1 *Billboard* chart hit "Deep Purple." It was the early days of the Righteous Brothers and we'd do tours together, we had a ball.

> **Nino Tempo**   I met Bill at an afternoon record hop in San Bernardino. April and I were promoting our first record on Atlantic, and on the drive there we were listening to the radio station that was hosting the hop. They said, "Here's the Righteous

Brothers' new record; they'll be at the hop along with Nino and April." Then they played "Little Latin Lupe Lu." I thought, "Wow they sound good, great R&B singers."

When April and I walked into the hop Bill and Bobby were singing. I was taken aback, "Holy cow, they're white guys!" Then April and I got up and did our new song, "Sweet and Lovely," and began a friendship with Bill that's now lasted over fifty years.

We went on tour with them and our first tour was fifty shows in just fifty-two days! Sometimes we'd take three flights in the same day and then rent a car and drive a hundred miles. It was trying but it was fun. One day at the hotel Bill was walking through the lobby and said, "Hey Nino, wanna join me for a beer in the bar?" I said, "Sure." We chatted for about twenty minutes and Bill said, "You know, I have a feeling maybe we could be good friends." I said, "Really? That's great, OK." We shook hands and our friendship has lasted since then without so much as a cross word.

After I'd become established in Vegas I wanted to help Nino and April get into the lounge at the Sands. I went with Nino and my road manager Mike Patterson to meet with Moe Lewis who, as you may remember from earlier in the book, was *the* guy when it came to booking the Sands. I was not particularly dressed well for such a meeting; I was wearing slippers, a ratty old sweater, and Levis. I also hadn't shaved for about three days, not exactly the look I wanted the "public" to see me in.

Anyway, we made the deal and noticed that Bobby Darin was playing at the Flamingo. Nino and Bobby were great friends so we decided to go see the show. We kind of snuck in the back because I was dressed so badly. About halfway through the show Bobby Darin stopped and said, "I have a friend here who just plays the crap out of the saxophone and he's had hit records with April Stevens—Nino Tempo, come on up Nino." (In addition to singing hit records Nino was one of the most sought after sax and clarinet players, a great all-around musician.)

Nino went up and he whispered in Bobby Darin's ear. All of a sudden Bobby announces, "Ladies and gentlemen, Bill Medley from the Righteous Brothers is here—Bill come on up." There was no way, dressed like I was, that I was going to get up there. I signaled a polite no thanks but they persisted. They started playing "What'd I Say" and stayed on that vamp for about three minutes while I kept saying, "No, no, thanks, but no!"

"C'mon up Bill Medley!" They wouldn't give up. Finally Mike Patterson said, "You're just gonna have to go up . . . and start dressing better." Finally I gave in. We had a pitcher of beer on the table and as I got up to go I nudged the table and the pitcher of beer spilled all over my crotch. Dressed like a homeless guy, with my pants looking like I'd just had a bladder accident, I took the stage in the main room at the Flamingo Hotel in Las Vegas. Since they were already playing the music I couldn't stop and explain what had happened. Thank God this was before cell phone cameras. After the song I tried to explain, "Bobby, sorry for the way I'm dressed, I was just coming into town for a quick meeting, and I spilled a pitcher of beer on my way up here." I'm not sure he even heard me because he was laughing so hard. Bobby Darin and Nino Tempo were just cracking up, along with the audience, as I sheepishly tried to explain my way out of that one.

I did learn a great lesson though. Believe me, I never go out in public looking like that anymore, and I'm extra careful about having pitchers of liquids on my table. In hindsight, it was one of my most embarrassing moments, but one of my funniest too. A great memory with great friends. I was always sad that we only got to keep Bobby Darin for thirty-seven years. One of the few things I loved about the Righteous Brothers' hit record "Rock and Roll Heaven" was that it has a tribute to Bobby Darin in the lyrics. No one deserves it more.

DR. JOHN

Yet another "foot in mouth" moment in my life. I was walking down the hall at a recording studio and I heard this great New Orleans funk coming out of studio B. I stopped to listen and heard this raspy-voiced singer just tearin' it up. I thought, "Damn, that's good!"

I poked my head into the control booth to see who it was and saw a friend of mine was producing. I went in and sat down and finally the guy who was singing came into the booth and my friend said, "Bill, I want you to meet Dr. John."

I'm like, "Oh shit, Dr. John—I love your stuff, so nice to meet you!"

He looked at me with puzzlement, "Bill, it's me."

I said, "Oh, I'm sorry—have we met?"

"Bill, I'm fuckin' Mac Rebennack!"

"Oh crap," I thought. Mac Rebennack played on a shitload of my records. He was part of the infamous "Wrecking Crew" studio group, and he used to drive down to Orange County to do other sessions for me. Fuckin' Mac Rebennack became Dr. John, the legendary singer–songwriter, boogie-woogie blues guy. Who knew?

That was yet another of my embarrassing, "nice to meet you" moments. Not long ago I had a forty-five-minute conversation with Mac in Vegas. Even though I could hardly understand a word through his thick New Orleans accent, I enjoyed it. Another great, talented guy.

GLEN CAMPBELL

Our first tour after "Lovin' Feelin'" went to #1 had two opening acts, Bobby Goldsboro and Glen Campbell. I've never heard so many corny jokes in my life; it never stopped. Bobby used to call Glen "helmet-head" because of the way he styled his hair, sprayed to a bullet-proof shine.

It was a very successful tour and this was the 1965 Glen Campbell, before he was, well, Glen Campbell. Same talent and style, but few outside of the studio musician crowd had heard of him. He'd do "It's Over" by Roy Orbison and just kill it, he was unbelievably good.

Five years later, when Glen became super huge with hit records, movies, and TV, we went on tour with him as *his* opening act. Glen is a funny guy. Here's a story that typifies Glen's humor. When we were opening for him, Bobby would leave the stage to catch his breath and I'd do my Ray Charles medley. "Born to Lose," "You Don't Know Me," and "I Can't Stop Loving You." I weave it together like a story and I just love doing it; I think that's what makes it work. One night I sang the heck out of it and the crowd was on their feet applauding and yelling. I walked offstage and Glen gave me a casual "OK" sign with his hand and said, "Nice try."

Glen was always great to us, having us on his TV show and doing whatever he could to help. It's been sad for me to watch him struggle with Alzheimer's. I saw him on TV last year, promoting his final tour. His wonderful wife Kim was with him and he'd have to turn to her to help him remember certain things and navigate the interview; it broke my heart.

I thought I'd better call him while I could. I expected his wife to answer but he did, "Hello, hello, hello!"

I said, "Glen? It's Medley."

"Bill, geez it's great to hear from you." He was just as fun and together as the old Glen had ever been, just perfect. After that I thought I'd back away, because that's how I want to remember Glen. I love the guy.

Everybody knew there was a problem the past few years because he'd forget stuff onstage and not do well communicating. People assumed it was a drug or alcohol thing. Glen's past struggles with substance abuse led people to that conclusion, but they were dead wrong.

A few years ago I was working in Branson with Paul Revere and the Raiders. My son Darrin was singing lead for them at the time. Glen came to town in a package show with (the late) Andy Williams, another of my all-time favorite people. Andy and Glen came to our show several times and we'd hang out afterwards. I told them I'd come to see them perform on Monday, my night off.

I went to see their show and I found it interesting that Andy introduced me while Glen was on the stage, like he was afraid Glen might have said, "Bill's here?" or "Who's Bill?" I went backstage afterwards and Glen gave me a huge hug and said, "Bill, what are you doin' in town?"

My heart sunk, but I knew then it had nothing to do with drugs or booze. In fact, during the times we'd hung out earlier that week Glen never even had a beer—nothing. I called my friend singer–songwriter Jim Stafford, who was big in Branson, and he told me, "Nobody's supposed to know this but Glen has a medical problem."

I'm glad Glen came "out of the closet" with his Alzheimer's struggle, if for no other reason than to shut up the press who always want to assume the worst so they can get a story. I'm sad for him and his family, but time will never take away the great memories. In case you read this Glen, I want to tell you one more time—I love you.

21 | Lights, Camera, Action

Movies and TV have had a tremendous impact on my career, way beyond the ones we've already talked about, *Shindig* and *Rambo*. I've actually been involved, in one way or another, in over thirty feature films and tons of TV shows too.

When our first hit records exploded, everything that you'd think was fantastic became the norm. Like, "OK, we're doing *The Ed Sullivan Show*, then Dean Martin, Danny Kaye, Bob Hope, *The Tonight Show*, etc."—the biggest TV shows of the day. We were running everywhere so I don't remember much, although I do remember singing with the great Peggy Lee on *The Ed Sullivan Show*, that was really cool for us.

One funny memory is the first time we did *American Bandstand* with Dick Clark. This was in the "Little Latin Lupe Lu" days, before we really hit it big. The show was still in Philadelphia then and when we got there they said, "OK you're gonna stand here."

I asked, "Where's the room? Where do we do the real show?"

"This is it," they said.

I couldn't believe how small it was because everything looks so big on TV.

Another show we loved to do was *The Lloyd Thaxton Show*, which was a local Los Angeles program on KCOP-TV. Lloyd was so hip, it was like the *American Bandstand* of Los Angeles and he loved R&B music. We just thought Lloyd was the coolest thing around; he was a real guy, not a "teeny-bopper" guy. Right before Bobby passed away in 2003 we worked the Hollywood Bowl. We got other "blue-eyed soul" singers and groups, like Felix Cavaliere from the Rascals, and Blood, Sweat and Tears on the show and we sold the place out—17,000 seats. When we were asked who should introduce us, Bobby said, "Do you think Lloyd Thaxton's still around?"

I said, "I don't know, but that would be perfect!"

Lloyd was still around and it was perfect because Bobby passed away right after. It was almost like Bobby knew, "Hey, I'm gettin' out of here," and that was a great way to go out.

TV exposure opened a lot of doors for us, but it was a stretch for me. With my anxiety struggles it was sometimes difficult because TV is "hurry up and wait." Like, "We don't need you for four hours, but be here just in case." I did have a couple opportunities to break out in starring roles though. I could have been Bronson, here's the story.

Just after I'd left the Righteous Brothers in 1968 I was signed to MGM Records. The guy they had to look after me, to make sure I wasn't spending too much of their money, was a sweet older man named Jessie Kaye. We became dear friends. He had a big MGM publicity picture of me on the wall in his office.

One day a guy walked in and said, "That is Bronson!"

"No, that's Bill Medley," said Jessie.

The guy said, "No, let me explain. I just wrote a television series called *Then Came Bronson* and that *is* Bronson. Are you tellin' me that's Bill Medley of the Righteous Brothers, with the low voice?"

"Yes."

"Do you think he would ride a motorcycle?"

Jessie knew everything about me and he said, "Are you kidding? Bill was raised riding motorcycles, he still races in scrambles."

The whole plot of *Then Came Bronson* was about this guy who leaves his corporate job to ride a motorcycle across the United States, it was perfect. The "guy" who was creating the show was Denne Bart Petitclerc, a guy with a foreign-sounding name who actually grew up in an orphanage in San Jose.

That night David Cohen, Jerry Perenchio, and Petitclerc came to Vegas to see me. I did some theatrical stuff in my show because I knew why they were there. Afterwards they came up to my suite and Petitclerc threw the manuscript on my bed and said, "Please, be Bronson."

"I've never really acted," I said.

He said, "I've seen you, you can act. You're a performer."

At that point Jerry Perenchio was still my agent but his company had grown so big that some other guy from his office took over the *Bronson* negotiations. Finally, I got a phone call.

"They don't want you, they want Michael Parks. NBC guaranteed the pilot would be made into a series if they used Michael Parks."

"Crap," I thought. That part would have been perfect for me—it felt so right. I didn't get it.

A couple years later I was at Jerry Perenchio's office coming down in the elevator. The guy next to me looked over and said, "You're Bill Medley."

"Yeah."

He said, "Do you remember me? I'm the guy who wrote *Then Came Bronson*."

I said, "Oh yeah, I'm sorry that didn't work out."

"We just couldn't afford it," he said.

I was puzzled, "Afford what?"

"What your agency was asking for you to do it," he said.

I was pissed. I never heard anything about a price—I would have done it for nothing. It turns out it wasn't Jerry, it was that other agent who worked for Jerry. I can't even remember his name, but he really screwed up the deal.

We stopped the elevator and went up to the top floor where they had a bar and ordered a couple drinks. Petitclerc was broken-hearted about it too. He told me even after they got Michael Parks they still wanted me. *Bronson* only lasted a year on NBC, but Petitclerc told me, "The show would still be on the air if you were *Bronson*. I wrote it for you. You *were* Bronson."

"I didn't know anything about any offers," I told him, and I could see him dying on the inside. It would have been huge for both of us. Michael Parks ended up having a couple hit records because he was on the show—you can imagine what it would have done for me.

As we sat there and talked we grew increasingly sick and pissed off. Years later I saw Petitclerc in Palm Springs. We had a couple beers and talked about how career-altering it would have been for both of us if our connection hadn't fizzled. He went on to have pretty good success in TV and the movies, but *Bronson* was his "baby." I'm not sure he ever got over missing what it could have been. He passed away in 2006.

Another role that could've been mine was in Andrew Lloyd Webber's *Jesus Christ Superstar*. I'd been asked to audition for the original Broadway play and I turned it down because I didn't want to go to New York and get tied up in a play. When they went to make the movie Andrew called and said he wanted me for the part of Jesus. I wasn't sure, but I thought I'd at least go audition.

I grew a Jesus-like beard and my bandleader Lee Ferrell learned one of the songs from the play and went with me. The film's director, Norman Jewison, was there with Andrew Lloyd Webber. I did the song in my key and Jewison stopped me, "Wait a minute. We need you to do this in the same key as the record from the play."

I said, "The guy who sang that was a first tenor, I can't hit those notes."

"We're going to do all the songs in the same key the album was made," he said.

"I can't do that, why didn't you tell me that?"

Jewison replied, "Well, they should have told you. Do you want to try out for the devil or something else?"

"No, I'm either Jesus or nobody," I said.

Norman Jewison was so sweet and apologetic, "I'm so sorry, someone should have told you."

As I walked away I said, "By the way, Mr. Jewison, Jesus was a baritone."

He laughed and said, "He probably was."

Growing my hair and beard out for the movie audition had an unintended negative consequence. A while earlier I had done a killer tour in Australia. I opened the first night just for the critics and the next day the reviews looked like my mom wrote them, just glowing. The next night you couldn't get into my show and they couldn't wait to have me back.

When I returned the reporters met me at the airport. The next day the papers were full of my picture with long hair and a beard with the headline, "Medley Became a Hippie." That was the end of my career in Australia. I tried to tell them I was just growing it out for the movie, but they ran with the hippie story anyway. In those days Australia was about ten years behind us and they weren't ready for a "hippie" Bill Medley. I went from hero to zero in Australia in one day over a beard I was growing for a movie audition. I never went back there until I did the *Dirty Dancing* movie tour. By then I guess all was forgiven because it went great.

In spite of a few bumps along the way, movies and TV have been pretty good to me. In 1990 I did a guest shot on the TV show *Cheers*. Kirstie Alley and Ted Danson are so darn funny—they made it easy for me. The episode was titled "Finally!" and it centered on Kirstie's relationship with her super-rich boyfriend Robin Colcord. Kirstie's character Rebecca finally got together with Robin and she told him that "You've Lost That Lovin' Feelin'" was the song that really pressed her romantic button. In response, Robin had a radio station he owned play it all night long and then sent me to *Cheers* to sing it to her in person.

All week long in rehearsal I'd done my lines perfectly, but when it came time to shoot the episode in front of a live audience I stumbled over the name Robin Colcord. Ted Danson, without skipping a beat, threw his arms out wide and said, "Oh great! Big fuckin' rock & roll star can't even say Robin Colcord." After a few tense moments he started laughing and the audience caught on that he was kidding. Later he told me everybody in that cast had screwed up that name at least once.

I asked Kirstie how they came to write that bit about "Lovin' Feelin'" into the plot. She told me that it really *was* the song that pushed her romantic button. She's a talented, funny lady— just like the character she played on the show. It's a great memory for me.

I have lots of great memories from working with gifted people in the TV and film industry. I sang on the soundtracks or did the theme songs for thirty-three movies and TV shows at last count.

Movies like *Major League,* Bruce Willis' *The Last Boy Scout, Top Gun, Ghost,* and of course *Dirty Dancing.*

I sang the theme song for a cute little sitcom on ABC called *Just the Ten of Us.* It was a spin-off of *Growing Pains* and has developed kind of a cult following since it went off. It lasted three seasons and won an Emmy, great show.

Once I did a TV pilot with George "Goober" Lindsay for a series called *Goober and the Truckers' Paradise.* It was set in a truck stop and I played a character called "Bible Bill," a very religious truck driver. I remember one line I had; it's always stuck with me. I was talking to a mechanic who was behaving badly and I said, "Wait a minute brother. When the Lord looks under the hood of your life are you gonna be a quart low?" The pilot aired once on CBS but wasn't picked up as a series. I had a lot of fun making it though.

From a career standpoint there are three movies that really kept me and the Righteous Brothers going for decades. The first was *Top Gun.* When Tom Cruise started singing "Lovin' Feelin'" in the bar scene, I knew it was going to be a great thing for us.

For some reason, somebody decided not to re-release "Lovin' Feelin'" after *Top Gun* was such a hit, which was weird to me. If they'd have released it, it would have gone to #1 again. They didn't even put it on the movie soundtrack, I have no idea why.

I know it would have been a smash because when I'd do my shows I'd see fifteen-year-old kids in the audience singing "Lovin' Feelin'" with me—right along with their parents. I asked how they knew it and they told me it was because of *Top Gun.* It opened up a new generation of fans for us.

Shortly after *Top Gun* came out I was asked to do another movie song, but I wasn't too excited about it. Remember, I'd just done the song for the Sylvester Stallone movie *Cobra*—the duet with Gladys Knight "Lovin' on Borrowed Time," which hadn't done anything.

I got a phone call from music producer Jimmy Ienner. "Bill, we're doing this movie and I want you to sing the title song for it."

I asked, "What's the movie?"

"*Dirty Dancing*."

"What?" I said, "It sounds like a bad porno movie."

Jimmy assured me, "Oh no, no, no—it's kind of a rock & roll thing."

I thought for a minute. "Well, who's in it?"

He told me Patrick Swayze and Jennifer Grey. Well, before *Dirty Dancing*, Patrick Swayze was not that well known.

Jimmy persisted. "You're the voice, you're the voice for Patrick and I need you to come to New York to do it." They wanted me to come right around the time my daughter McKenna was going to be born.

I told him, "I can't do it. Not only do I not want to do it, I can't do it because I promised Paula I'd be there when our child was born."

They wouldn't hear no. They sent me the song and again, like with "Lovin' Feelin'," they had the guy on the demo singin' real high. I gotta tell you, I just wasn't crazy about the song, not for me at least. I knew it was a good song, but a good Bill Medley song? I didn't think so.

But this guy stayed after me, he'd call me about every week. "Bill, we can come there, whatever."

I held my ground. "No, I'm not gonna do it."

Finally, McKenna was born, and they called again and said Jennifer Warnes would do it if she could do it with me. She'd just had a monster hit duet with Joe Cocker, "Up Where We Belong."

I always thought that was a great pairing, kind of a Beauty and the Beast thing. Kind of like John Wayne being with Marie Osmond—something like that.

Jennifer Warnes I instinctively knew our voices would be complimentary and was curious about the song Jimmy Ienner had in mind. During that period I had been the singer of Oscar-nominated songs and two had actually won, so I knew if I partnered with Bill Medley we would need a very strong song. When the demo arrived I was hopeful when I placed it in the cassette player, but as the song finished I fell silent. My boyfriend, who was listening too, spoke first.

"Has the company offered you a decent fee, Jenny?"

"Yes."

He said, "Well, maybe you can accept it for that reason or for the fun of singing with Bill Medley—but no one will ever hear this song." I still have that cassette; I play it now and then to savor the joke.

For me, I had simply wanted to sing with Bill Medley since I was a teenager. When I was a sad, fatherless freshman in glasses, carrying heavy geometry books, my school bus passed a creepy frontage road with a broken down dance bar called the Flamingo. Ford Fairlanes and Chrysler Imperials crammed the fields nearby whenever the marquee read *Righteous Brothers—Tonight!* I wish someone had tapped me on the shoulder then and whispered, "Don't worry honey, one day you'll sing with that tall, sexy one and everything will turn out just fine."

I went up to the studio and learned it enough to throw a bunch of stuff on about 15 tracks. Jennifer and I were trading melody and harmony lines, answers, shouting lines, lots to choose from. "There you go," I said, and we left.

Fast-forward a few weeks, and I'm on the road with the Righteous Brothers. The local radio station was going to introduce us that night, and the DJ pulled me aside and said, "Man, we're playing the hell outta your record."

I said, "What record?"

He shot back, "You know, the record from the movie—you're singin' with the girl."

I figured it was the record with Gladys Knight from the Stallone movie and thought, "Oh, cool!" and didn't give it much more thought.

When I got home I found out it was the song from *Dirty Dancing*. I took Paula to the movie and, sure enough, there it was right in the right spot of the movie. I think kids were running out of the theater to buy the album. The album sold over thirty-two million copies and the single was #1 all over the world. This was the song I turned down for three months. It really was great for me personally and continued to give me a life apart from my identity as a Righteous Brother, which was important to me at that time.

In 1990 the movie *Ghost* came out, which featured our song "Unchained Melody." I told David Cohen we should call Mike Curb to see if we could get it re-released. Mike was the young "whiz-kid" of the music business. He owned Curb records, launched dozens of careers, was made president of MGM while in his early twenties and eventually became lieutenant governor of California. Just a brilliant guy.

He said there was a problem releasing "Unchained Melody" again because of some leasing rights issue. However, Mike had an idea, "I'll tell you what, go back in the studio and record it again."

Bobby wasn't really in "Unchained Melody" shape, at least not to record it like the original with all those high notes—but, we went in the studio anyway and I worked with him and we got it. Not as good as the original but close enough, we captured as much of the magic as we could.

We released it and it sold like crazy. That inspired us to re-record a whole "reunion" album of our hits. Honestly, it was shit. It was a stupid thing to do because you can never really remake those records. It was just that we'd given away all of our rights and this was a way to get them back. Artistically, a stupid idea; financially, a wonderful idea. The album went platinum.

Then a weird thing happened. Two separate versions of "Unchained Melody," the original and our "reunion" version, hit the *Billboard* top 15 at the same time. *Billboard* bases their charts on airplay and sales. The original was getting the airplay but when the kids went to the record stores to buy it, Curb had flooded them with our "reunion" version. He pressed half a million copies in advance! Our version eventually sold a million singles and the album sold a million copies too.

With three big movie songs in four years we were hot as ever—to our older fans and now a whole new generation of kids. I got a call from David Cohen who told me the William Morris Agency was offering twenty thousand dollars a night for as many dates as we wanted. I said, "No, I'm gonna stay as Bill Medley. "

Even though I had technically reunited with Bobby I still worked a lot on my own and wasn't ready to commit as a Righteous Brother. It wasn't an anti-Bobby thing; I really enjoyed performing on my own. I got to do the Righteous Brothers' songs and my own stuff too.

A week later David called back, "They're offering twenty-five thousand a night."

I said, "No."

David called again, "They're up to thirty thousand a night; think about it."

"No thanks."

He kept calling and the price kept going up: forty thousand, fifty, then sixty thousand a night.

I said, "You mean they can book us on tour for sixty thousand a night? I'll take it."

That was really the first time in my life, at least in my mind, that I ever committed to being a Righteous Brother. Bobby and I had never sat down and said, "Let's be the Righteous Brothers." It just happened. Even though I was earning huge money working with Bobby, I still wasn't committed. In some ways I was taking advantage of the situation, trying to get by on the cheap without a sound or light guy, cutting corners.

This time I wanted to lay all the cards on the table, I sat down with Bobby and our bandleader Barry Rillera and laid everything out. "Here's the deal, here's what we can get and here's what we can do." I wanted to do it right. After all our success, from 1962 on, I never truly committed to being a Righteous Brother until 1990. From then on a new world opened up for me.

22 | From Dogshit to Diamonds

As I've shared, the 1970s were not good for me. I was in a bad place mentally, Karen was murdered and I had to grow up fast to raise Darrin. I had opened my first restaurant, Medley's, and it was losing a couple hundred thousand a year, and I went through the bad breakup with Janice—it was painful. Then the 1980s hit and my world began to turn from dogshit to diamonds. I converted Medley's to The Hop—a rock & roll-themed nightclub with a killer show called *Rock Around the Clock*. It went from being a money-loser to making three hundred grand a year profit.

The Hop concept and the *Rock Around the Clock* show were perfect for that time in Orange County. In the early 1980s the TV show *Happy Days* was still going strong on ABC and the nostalgia thing was a hit with the prime nightclub age crowd. Our target audience was the forty-year-old woman; I wanted them to feel real comfortable, not like a meat market. Like, you went to a regular nightclub to get laid—but you went to The Hop to find someone to marry; it was that kind of atmosphere. Over the years, dozens of married couples have come up to me and told me they met there.

Not long ago at a show in Lake Tahoe a guy yelled out from the audience, "I met my wife at The Hop." Then another couple yelled out the same thing, then another! Three couples in just that one show had met at The Hop—pretty cool.

We had the place set up like a high school gymnasium; the dance floor was a basketball court complete with the rims and balloons—just like a senior prom every night. Bobby and I worked there once a month, and we'd bring in other rock & roll stars too, but the real attraction was the show. Some of my friends were skeptical and I understood why. I mean, a Vegas production show in a 5,000-square-foot gym in Fountain Valley, California? I produced it and it featured some of the best musicians, singers, and dancers around. We had a killer band, three girl and four guy singers, and a great disc jockey to set the mood before and after. We also had a terrific comedian, Jason Chase, who was so funny and clean, he was the perfect fit. I was really proud of it—the performers blew the crowds away.

Rock Around the Clock performer and musical director Bobby Cruz   It was standing room only for the first five years. If you didn't get there by six for the eight o'clock show you didn't get a seat. There was nothing like it in Southern California, it was more of a Vegas-style show. I'd never done anything like it; I'd never even seen anything like it.

The energy of the show was on full blast for an hour and twenty minutes. Bill found great people to perform and he knew what he wanted. From the very beginning he was right there, hands on, changing anything that didn't work. He had all the musical ideas—what songs to put where and how to hook them together. He knew exactly what he was looking for.

When the first musical director Larry Hanson left Bill hired me to write the charts. I'd go to his house and we'd sit down at the piano and he'd say, "Yeah that's good" or "That doesn't work, let's do this." It was an incredible learning experience for me.

Bill also got me to do something I never thought I could. I'd always sung behind my keyboard, since I was fourteen. He got me out in front singing and dancing—and I was scared to death! Bill had a great way of making everyone feel relaxed and pumping them up. We felt so comfortable, it wasn't even like work.

Once, on my birthday, I was singing a solo in the middle of the show and all of a sudden loud recorded music came on and the band stopped. My mind was swimming and I didn't know what to do. It turned out it was a birthday song and everyone started pointing at me. Bill came walking out from the wings and grabbed me by the back of the head and kissed me smack on the lips—in front of a packed house of 800 people. The band started laughing, so did I. It was hilarious, the audience ate it up. That's how it was working for Bill, he wasn't afraid to show emotion.

I mentioned our comedian in the show, Jason Chase. Prior to working in *Rock Around the Clock* Jason had mostly been a guitar player and singer who did cute little bits in between songs with props. Somehow, I just knew that Jason was the guy who could do stand-up for fifteen minutes in the middle of a sizzling show and leave the crowd pumped for the finish—he was great.

Comedian Jason Chase   I really didn't know what Bill wanted at first, he just said, "Show up and be cute." The first day of rehearsal it dawned on me that he wanted a comedian and that was something new for me. I'd always had my guitar to hide behind, it was like my shield. It turned out to be the perfect job for me though and started me on a whole new career path.

Those were the days when Jerry Seinfeld and other clean comedians were becoming popular and that really worked for me. As the show began to succeed, my new career as a comic took off. I started opening for Captain & Tennille, Melissa Manchester, Waylon Jennings and, of course, the Righteous Brothers. Then I started working as a headliner on cruise ships—forty weeks a year for the next twenty years! That all happened because Bill Medley took a chance on me.

The audiences at The Hop got to be my friends. They really helped me and my wife Tricia when she was diagnosed with stage four cancer. We still stay in touch with many of them, we're like family. Bill was great during that time as well; he's a good guy and a good friend.

Things started to blossom. My then-girlfriend Paula was involved in everything; she designed The Hop and ran it like a pro. She's sharp, no one can put anything over on her, and she calls it like she sees it. There were lines out the door to get in.

Paula Medley   After going through a couple of other managers Bill's partners in The Hop came to me and asked me to manage the place. I'd been involved in the restaurant business for years but I was thinking, "This could be tough, everybody's gonna think I manage here because I date Bill."

It was a phenomenon. It was like a train that left the station and I got to drive it; it was exciting. When I got pregnant with McKenna I decided to leave but I didn't want to. Since I'd been there at the start and done the décor and planning with Bill it felt kind of like "our baby."

I met Paula when she was about twenty-three; she was a waitress and kind of a little "hippie chick." Long blond curly hair, a great figure, and just beautiful. I asked her out and she said, "No."

I thought, "Wait a minute, do you know who I think I am?" I was a legend in my own mind.

I think she was going with some guy then, but I persisted. I asked her out three or four times and she still said no. Finally I said, "My son Darrin is having a birthday—would you go out to dinner with us to celebrate?"

"Your son's going? OK."

We picked her up in my two-seater Ferrari, Darrin had to straddle the shifter for us to fit. We had a great time and that was how Paula and I got started. We dated for a while and I started doing my normal "on and off" crap. I'd tell her I thought we needed to stop seeing each other then a month later there I was, "I'm back!"

Thankfully, Paula hung in there through all my coming and going. In 1985 when I opened The Hop we really connected. She was the one who really made that place go and I should mention that her brother, Mark Vasu, was also instrumental in designing the floor plan. He did a great job; he managed it for a while and then went on to create a very successful chain called Blue Martini. While we were building The Hop we'd have dinner every night, real late after the work was done. I think that's when Paula and I really came together for good.

At the same time The Hop exploded I began opening for the group Alabama. I did that for a year, and the money was coming in from all sides, I could feel every part of my life beginning to come together. When I'd come back to Orange County I'd stay with Paula, she lived in a little apartment over the Orange Julius in Balboa. Here I was, I owned this wildly successful nightclub (thanks to Paula) and I was opening for one of the hottest acts in the country at the time, and I'd come home to a cramped apartment over the Orange Julius. Then I got an offer to sub (with Bobby, as the Righteous Brothers) for Siegfried and Roy, the famous magicians, at the Frontier Hotel in Vegas. We did incredible business there and that was the start of the Righteous Brothers "main-room" Vegas success that continued from the 1980s until Bobby's death in 2003. The 1980s were night and day compared to the 1970s—everything was going great.

Paula and I had always said we'd get married if she got pregnant. One day she called me in Vegas, she was crying—she was pregnant. I know she assumed that meant I'd be gone, doing my Bill Medley thing like, "I'll send you some money, but I'm gone."

I think I surprised her when I said, "This is great! When I get home we'll get married."

"You're kidding."

I said, "Nope, I mean it."

At first Paula wasn't too sure. She's a smart lady and let's face it, my track record in marriage hadn't been that great. Eventually, we decided it was what we wanted—we got married in July of 1986. Even then, somewhere in my brain I thought, "I'll probably be around a year or two and then I'll be gone." Wrong—at the time of this writing we've been married twenty-seven years!

I'd always wanted a baby girl. We went for an ultrasound, and a few days later the nurse called and asked me if I wanted to know the baby's sex. I kind of didn't, but I was also kind of chicken shit so I said, "Yeah, I would."

"It's a girl."

I just started yelling at the top of my lungs. I couldn't believe it. I called Paula at The Hop and said with a teasing tone, "I know what it is, I know what it is. . ."

Paula was seven days overdue so I knew we were pretty close. I was at The Hop and Roy Orbison was our guest star that night. Roy was really struggling at that time and I was backstage talking with him wondering if he was going to be able to pull off all those high notes in his hits. I thought, "Man, I'm not sure if I can even watch this, it could be brutal." Then he took the stage and hit everything, just like the records, it blew me away.

As Roy was hitting high gear the bartender came and got me, "Paula's on the phone."

"Tell her I'll call back."

He said, "No, it's important."

I got on the phone and asked her what was so important.

"My water just broke," she said.

Just for a moment I weighed in my mind, "Let's see, should I watch Roy Orbison or take Paula to the hospital." Of course, I ran home and took her to the hospital. I was in the room with her as the docs did the C-section. Paula hates pain; she takes a Valium to get her teeth cleaned, so they had her pretty numbed up.

I tried to encourage her, "You're doing great." All of a sudden they cut the cord and baby McKenna started crying. I can't explain it. It was like electricity zapped right into my heart and soul. Not that I didn't have similar feelings when Darrin was born, but I was a different guy then and this was a new and powerful thing—it just floored me. I've never been right since; I still have the same feelings today. McKenna is a great singer and performer and works with me all the time. When I look across the stage my heart still jumps like it did twenty-six years ago in the delivery room.

Maybe it's because I'm older and a little wiser, but my commitment level to McKenna and Paula is light years ahead of what it was when I was young. The twenty-five-year-old Bill Medley and the forty-five-year-old Bill Medley who married Paula were two different guys.

Paula Medley   It's always been fun to be married to Bill. It's an interesting life; we never know what's coming around the corner. People ask me why we've lasted so long and I'm not exactly sure, but I remember when I was very young and we were dating. He was in a little faster lane back then and I always thought, "I wouldn't mind waiting until I'm about thirty-five and he's forty-five and then we'll get together." Like, we'd both sow our oats by then and be more serious. I always thought we'd eventually get together and as it turned out that's exactly what happened.

Even though I turned him down a few times before I decided to date him I always liked him, Bill was charming from the get-go. My sister always tells me how lucky I am to be married to someone who's so much fun. Bill really does have a great sense of humor, he makes everything fun. Another thing I love is that he's a stand-up guy. I feel so secure with him, I always trust him to do the right thing.

Paula is just the best. For one thing, she gives me the space to have what I call "buffoon time" with my buddies from high school. But the big thing is, I love Paula. I'm really *in* love with Paula. I don't know any other way to explain it. Nobody's more surprised than me and my old friends that I'm still here. She's smart, artistic and it's the first time I've ever been with someone who I can be alone with for a month and have a great time. We love to go to dinner and watch movies together. Believe me, she's who you want in the foxhole with you when the bullets start flying. I'm going to grow old and die on the porch with Paula, period.

23 | The Beat Goes On

After Paula and I built The Hop into a money-maker David Cohen really began to hit his stride as the Righteous Brothers agent/manager and all-around advocate. As I've shared, David is like my soulmate, I love the guy—but we're different. I don't really care for the hardball negotiations that are part of show business, but David is a master deal-maker.

You may have heard the term "four-wall" in association with Las Vegas performers. When an artist or group "four-walls" a room they basically take all the ticket sales and return a percentage to the house. If you do great business you make a fortune, if you don't you die. Today most of the major showrooms in Las Vegas are booked that way. The casinos love it because their risk is minimal and if it works they get a house full of energized gamblers before and after the show. David Cohen was one of the first guys to bring the four-wall concept to Vegas.

We'd been doing great business at the old MGM (now Bally's), and when they built the new MGM in 1993 we opened in their main room, the Hollywood Theatre. It was a great venue, it seated 1,400 and we'd sell out every night, twice on Saturdays. The whole hotel was massive; at the time it opened it was the largest hotel in the world—thirty floors in the main building containing 6,852 rooms and a 171,000-square-foot casino area. Nineteen restaurants, a convention center, an outdoor arena, shops, and a theme park, all on over six acres of prime Las Vegas Strip real estate. The whole town was buzzing about it.

When David went in to make the deal for us he asked to see the sleeping rooms we'd be given, he was told we'd be given suites. When the MGM staff showed David our suites he said, "No, this won't do." God bless David Cohen. If I ever needed someone to be the "bad cop" or make the unpleasant phone call I'd call David. He's just not afraid to tell anyone what he wants for his artists.

So, they moved up to the next level suite.

"Nope, this isn't good enough for my guys," he said. You're gonna have to show me your best suite."

They said they had the twenty-ninth floor, but it was reserved for the super high-rollers, guys who'd drop millions in gambling losses. David said, "Let me see those." They took him there and David said, "Now we're talking."

Now we're talking—I guess so. Each suite was 3,000 square feet, complete with an elevator and a dedicated chef. I could hardly believe David got them to give us those rooms; usually there would be someone like the Prince of Brunei staying on the twenty-ninth floor. Because we worked there so often I got to know the chefs and I felt kind of like a prince. I'd call them, "Hey, that one spaghetti thing you did, can you fix me one of those?" Boom, a few minutes later it's delivered.

Managers come and go in this business, but there are very few David Cohen-type guys who will go to bat for you like that. I would have settled for the first or second suite they offered and been happy about it, but not David. He just isn't afraid to ask for the best deal for his guys.

Because of David and Jerry Perenchio, the "second coming" of the Righteous Brothers was a financial bonanza for us. As I've shared, Bobby was almost homeless when David and I plucked him out of his Costa Mesa apartment in 1974, and through the 1980s, 1990s, and up until Bobby's passing in 2003, I was able to recoup the money I'd pissed away from our first successes.

We were really rolling in the 1980s in the main rooms of Las Vegas. We did killer business for the casinos, and Bobby and I were beginning to find a peace about working together. We had some great opening acts too, including a couple of comedians you may have heard of, Jay Leno and Brad Garrett. They were both wonderful guys who fit right in to our world—regular guys, real guys.

Brad Garrett Our first gig together was at the Desert Inn, one of the last really great hotels in Vegas, about 1986 or 1987. I was a big fan of soul music so to get to share the stage with them was a dream come true. I was also opening for Sinatra, Sammy Davis, Liza Minnelli, and Julio Iglesias at the time, but what really stood out for me about Bobby and Bill was that I immediately became part of the family. They were just amazingly gracious and kind. When you're an opening act your job is to just do your thing and give everybody their space, but they had their arms wide open from the beginning, they really took me in. I toured on and off with them until I got the *Everybody Loves Raymond* pilot,

I guess we were together for six or seven years, which is really unusual in this business.

Their audiences were the best. There's nothing like baby-boomer audiences for a comic, and Bill and Bobby gave me the freedom to experiment and really develop my stand-up stuff. We were always playing practical jokes on each other. I did a Bill Medley impression in my act and a bit about how his voice was so low that someday he'd lose one of his testicles in the middle of a show. Bill is so humble and has such a great sense of humor about himself. There are very few stars you can make fun of when you're opening for them.

We'd always go out to a famous Vegas steak house after the shows and everything was just loaded with garlic. One night we walked out talking about how bad our breath was and that if we breathed on someone they might die from garlic poisoning. The next night when I walked onstage someone had taped a little spray container of Binaca breath spray to my microphone. It was taped with duct tape; I couldn't even get it off. That kind of joking between the opening act and stars is pretty rare.

When you see how Bill treats the crew, the sound guys, and his band—that really tells you who he is. I mean, he's had some of the same guys playing with him for thirty years, that's all you need to know. He's a rare man with no pretense and he absolutely loves what he does. I love him. There are a lot of celebrities today but very few "stars" left. What makes a star, to me, is the relationship they have with the public. Bill came up the old school way and he's the same guy on and offstage. It wasn't the "Self-Righteous Brothers," it was the Righteous Brothers.

Brad Garrett is such a great person; he was with us for so long he really became part of the family. In many ways Brad is like a big kid, so much fun to be around. Because he's so much younger than Bobby and I we felt like he was our little brother, our 6'8" "little" brother. He used to joke that he had to buy shoes from the oversized displays in store windows because his feet were so big, and they really were.

When he got *Everybody Loves Raymond* we were thrilled for him but also really sad to see him go. He got very emotional when he told us, so did we. We threw a big going away party, and because of his ongoing jokes about his big feet Paula went out and bought him the biggest tennis shoes she could find, size seventeen I think. We filled them with $5 chips from the casino and attached a note saying, "Nobody can fill your shoes." That's true, nobody could. Brad Garrett is a one-of-a-kind, special guy.

Along with the great opening acts we had during the 1980s and 1990s, we also had terrific musicians in our band. Our keyboard player eventually became our road manager and musical director—a great musician and great guy, Lee Ferrell. Of course today, Lee is better known as Will Ferrell's dad. Lee had come to California from North Carolina and made quite a reputation for himself as a soulful organ and piano player. For years he was the solid glue that held the music together and an important part of the Righteous Brothers family.

Lee Ferrell   Bill always knew what he wanted musically. I learned a lot by watching him and listening to him, after a while I felt like we had a connection between what he was delivering and what I was playing. I knew what he was doing and where he wanted to go.

Bill's one of the great blues singers and, as a musician and singer myself, I learned a lot of the good stuff I know from him. Really, there's hardly a blues lick I do that hasn't been influenced by him. He's a really funny guy too. When they were young my sons Will and Patrick used to travel around with us and watch from the wings. Will told me he got a lot of good timing and delivery notes from watching Bill handle the audience and transition between songs.

When Will made his big debut on *Saturday Night Live* we all got together to watch. David Cohen, Bill, Brad Garrett, and a few of the band members came. I was very anxious because I wanted him to do well; I spent the whole show pacing back and forth in the room. They all started making fun of me because every time Will would come on-screen I'd run to the TV and point him out, "There's my son, there's Will—look at Will!" Bill was like, "Lee, we've known him since he was nine, we recognize him."

Brad Garrett   I think Will Ferrell did three scenes that night on *Saturday Night Live*, and I looked at Lee and told him he could retire. I knew Will was gonna be one of the biggest comedic stars ever.

He was brilliant right out of the gate. So many
people have to develop, I had to develop on
Everybody Loves Raymond, but Will was just
ready. When he came on it was magic.

Things were really rolling in the 1980s. Country music was
becoming really popular and since I'd always loved country music I
thought this would be the perfect time to do an album. I went to
Nashville and recorded what I thought was a pretty good record; the
title track from the album, "I Still Do," charted at #17 on the *Billboard* Country charts in June of 1984. I discovered, however, that
with all the success the Righteous Brothers had, Nashville was still
kind of an island unto itself. My personal manager at the time, Judi
Barlowe Fields, did the groundwork to open the doors.

Judi Barlowe Fields   As it turned out a lot of
the Nashville artists of that day were doing the kind
of music that would really fit Bill. There was Ronnie
Milsap, Barbara Mandrell, Alabama, Lee Greenwood,
Vince Gill, and Amy Grant—not twangy country at
all. That's where Bill's fans had migrated to.

Bill always had a fantasy of signing with RCA,
mainly because he and Elvis had been such good
friends and that was Elvis' label. I called them and
we set an appointment with their president Joe
Galante. The meeting went great and Bill said it felt
right. RCA said they had several producers they
could recommend but asked Bill who he thought
was making good records, thinking they'd find a
good match that way. He said, "Alabama, Lee

Greenwood, and Gary Morris." I set up meetings with their producers and when we got to Nashville our first meeting was with Harold Shedd, who was producing Alabama at the time.

When we walked into his office the secretary greeted us with typical southern charm, "Hi y'all, can I get you anything? Mr. Medley, anything at all?"

"No thanks, we're good."

Finally we went into his office, "Mr. Shedd, hi, I'm Judi Fields, thanks for seeing us—say hello to Bill Medley."

He said, "Hi Bill, good to meet you—so now Bill, what do you do?"

Bill looked at me, half-puzzled and half-amused and said, "Well Harold, I'm a singer."

"Well Bill, are you with any groups? Have you been out there? What kind of singin' do you do?" he asked.

I'm thinking, "Oh shit, what the hell do I do now?" Bill continued, "I'm kind of a rock & roll singer."

"Yeah? Have you ever had any records, Bill?"

"Oh, a couple—way back in the day. I sang with a group."

Harold said, "Anybody I might have heard of?"

I'm dying. Bill told him he was one of the Righteous Brothers and Harold said excitedly, "I've heard of them—which one were you?"

Without skipping a beat Bill said, "I'm the short, cute blond."

> When we got out of there I thought Bill was
> going to kill me but he was laughing so hard he
> couldn't be mad. The guy was as sweet as could be,
> but he didn't have a clue who Bill was.

In spite of that, my RCA country album got made and, as I shared, it had pretty good success. I was honored to be nominated by the Academy of Country Music for Best New Vocalist of the Year, even though I lost to this other guy you may have heard of—Vince Gill. All the while I was still working with Bobby as the Righteous Brothers, doing solo gigs, and The Hop was going strong.

Another really cool thing, and one that was not so cool, happened in the 1980s. I was diagnosed with prostate cancer. Jerry Perenchio, God bless him, sent me to the best guy—Dr. Jean DeKernion at UCLA. They were just starting to learn how to treat prostate cancer in those days. Because Jerry had made the call they met me at the front door and walked me through the whole process. Dr. DeKernion asked if I wanted to do the "seeding" technique that they were experimenting with at the time but I told him, "Just cut me open and get that shit out of me."

He asked, "Do you want to know what we're going to do?"

I said, "Absolutely not! Once I'm out you can take my head off if you need to, just put it back on before I wake up."

I had the operation and it was a success. Shortly after we got a call saying that Bill Clinton wanted us to sing at his Georgetown University alumni reunion at the White House. President Clinton was, apparently, a big Righteous Brothers fan. It was scheduled for the end of May, just a few weeks after my surgery. I was still struggling with bladder control, I don't know if they hit a nerve or what, but it was a problem.

Nevertheless, we went to Washington and met the president and first lady. I didn't know what to think about Hillary because she looked a little tough to me. Boy was I wrong; she was so sweet and wonderful to us. McKenna was just a little kid, Bobby brought his kids along too, and they took pictures with us all.

> **Paula Medley** We got to the hotel and they gave us an envelope with a White House seal and an invitation for pictures in the Oval Office. When we got there one of the Secret Service guys took us on a private tour and he told us stories about each of the rooms and what had happened in it—he even let us sit on the furniture, which I don't think he was supposed to do. As a mom I was so excited for McKenna to experience all of that.

Talk about charisma, when President Clinton walked in the oval office he was bigger than life. He told me, "Bill I just love the Righteous Brothers." He had a little cut over his eyebrow and, sure enough, Bobby just couldn't let it go, "What'd you do, cut yourself shaving?" The president laughed it off, he was a great sport. In the afternoon, when the band was doing sound check, he was out on the lawn practicing his putting. He stopped, came inside, and talked with the band for half an hour. We asked if he wanted to play sax but he politely refused, "If it was a concert maybe, but these are the kids I went to school with."

Both President and Mrs. Clinton spoke that night and then everyone started dancing on this huge dance floor they'd built. The Clintons worked their way around the floor to where they were dancing directly in front of us. We were singing "You'll Never Walk

Alone" and I'll never forget that President Clinton was singing right along with us, *When you walk through a storm, keep your head up high*—literally five feet from me. I held the microphone out to see if he wanted to sing but he backed away. It was so cool, even though I was wearing a diaper because of the bladder control thing. The Righteous Brothers were never really political at all; we were just honored to be performing for our president and first lady.

The 1980s and 1990s were a good time for me, especially into the 1990s when I'd finally figured out how to work with Bobby. As I've said, we were two really different guys, and once I resigned myself to not expect more from Bobby than he was capable of giving, emotionally that is, I was able to enjoy the many good parts of his personality and talent. I did worry about Bobby, we all did. He just wouldn't take care of himself and sometimes he was his own worst enemy.

Once we were performing in Reno, and Bobby began to complain that his leg was hurting. David Cohen kept asking what was wrong and Bobby would say, "Oh, I don't know, it'll go away." After one show his leg was so swollen that David emphatically told him, "We have to have someone look at that leg!" David literally forced him to go to the emergency room and it turned out he had a blood clot in his leg. They told us he could have easily died. They put him in the hospital and I flew to Vegas for a show the next night by myself. After a while the hospital started calling David to say Bobby was OK and it was time for him to leave—Bobby didn't want to go home.

I called Bobby and said I was coming up to pick him up and when we got there I told him, "You've been in here three weeks; they said you were healed a couple weeks ago—you gotta leave."

He said, "I don't wanna go." He was like a little boy.

I asked why he wanted to stay and he said, "Look, I push this button and they come in and ask what I want. I push this one and they bring me dinner. I push this and it gives me a dose of painkillers, this button turns on the TV—why would I want to leave here?"

We finally convinced him to go. He didn't have health insurance but the hospital agreed to cut the bill in half if he paid cash, which he did. We peeled him out of the bed but he was kickin' and screamin' the whole time—he *really* didn't want to leave. It was kind of funny but he was dead serious, he loved it there.

After Bobby recovered we continued headlining all over Vegas and many of the guys we'd grown up with in Vegas in 1965 were now running the hotels and casinos. One of those guys is my friend Michael Gaughan. Michael's father was Vegas legend Jackie Gaughan, who was there at the beginning, owning pieces of the Flamingo, El Cortez, Golden Nugget, Union Plaza, the Showboat, and many others. Michael grew up in the business and eventually owned many of the top Vegas casinos himself, including the Barbary Coast, the Suncoast, and the Orleans. He currently owns the South Point Hotel and Casino and all the slot machines at Vegas' McCarran International Airport.

Michael's a real guy's guy—he's into riding horses and was a race car driver—he won the big off-road race, the Mint 400, in 1966. He actually owned a NASCAR racing team for many years with his son Brendan as the driver. I love working at his hotels.

Michael Gaughan My relationship with the Righteous Brothers goes back to my childhood, literally. I first met them when they were appearing at the Sands in the 1960s—I've known Bill for almost fifty years, but we really became close friends about twenty years ago. He's always been a good guy, a fun guy to be around.

Bill and I had lots of good times. When we were young we drank and chased skirts a bit—it was wild in Vegas in those days; the town was a lot smaller. When I hit thirty I started growing up, we've kind of mellowed together.

Bill and Bobby used to work for me at the Orleans; they'd play about eight weeks a year. I used a lot of the acts from the 1960s at the Orleans—Little Richard, Dion, Frankie Avalon, Bobby Rydell, Bo Diddley, and the Everly Brothers. They were all great, but the Righteous Brothers drew better than anyone. I've never stopped using Bill at my hotels, even since Bobby passed away—Bill's a great entertainer.

I don't think you'll ever hear anybody knock Bill. With him it's what you see is what you get— no hidden agenda. He never says no to a fan and I've never had a harsh word with him.

The seeds we'd planted in our early days in Vegas and the relationships I'd built there after I left Bobby in 1968 really paid off in the Righteous Brothers "second life." Just as Jerry Perenchio had told me, if we were a hit when we went into Vegas with "Lovin' Feelin'" we'd have a place to perform for life.

Another thing that really helped us in Vegas in the 1980s and 1990s was that our core audience, the kids who were teens in the 1960s, had now grown into their 30s and 40s—just perfect for Vegas fun, gambling, and excitement. They had money to spend and weren't shy about it. That made us very popular with the hotels and casinos.

The last fifteen years I had with Bobby were the best fifteen years with Bobby. We were working all the time, the band was great, and the show was fun. As I talked about before, that's the time when I really committed to being a Righteous Brother and we kind of cruised through the 1990s on auto-pilot. Then in 2003, we hit a career milestone that turned out to be close to the finish line, we just didn't know it.

24 | The Hall

The Rock and Roll Hall of Fame in Cleveland has a pretty loose criteria for who gets in. Supposedly, you have to be around for twenty-five years and have made some sort of difference in the industry or the music. It doesn't seem like they've always followed that, if that was their criteria we should have gotten in long before we did. We felt like we were never going to get in so we pretty much said, "Who gives a shit?"

That is, until they called us and told us we were nominated in 2003. I'll never forget, I was in my bedroom when David Cohen called with the news and I shouted, "Yeah!" David told me to calm down; we were just nominated, not in yet. I was thinking, "Finally, they must have gotten to the "Rs" for Righteous Brothers."

We went in on the first ballot, but we were still a little puzzled about why it took so many years. Billy Joel, who inducted us, even commented about that in his speech. It was a lot of people's opinion that Phil Spector didn't want any of his acts in the Hall of Fame because that would have meant they were great artists, not just Spector puppets. Phil was very involved in the Hall of Fame, he had power there. He didn't want the Ronettes, or us, or Darlene Love in. Interestingly, since Phil got in trouble in 2003, we've all gone in—the Righteous Brothers, then the Ronettes, and finally Darlene Love. It kind of makes you wonder. When we got there for the ceremony Billy Joel, Sting, and Elton John were backstage. They all hugged Bobby and me and said, "Man, this is way overdue," every one of them. Billy Joel's induction speech was just great—it was seven minutes long! I couldn't have been more proud. Here are a few kind words from his speech:

> **Billy Joel**   I don't understand how these guys
> aren't in the Rock and Roll Hall of Fame already.
> The year was 1965. My friends and I were about
> sixteen years old when "You've Lost That Lovin'
> Feelin'" started getting airplay in the New York
> area. Bill Medley's bass register lead grabbed us
> immediately, and Bobby Hatfield's tenor responses
> were the perfect foil . . . sometimes, people with
> blue eyes transcend the limitations of what their
> color and their culture is supposed to be. Some-
> times white people can actually be soulful. This
> was a life-changing idea; it changed my life. Ladies
> and gentlemen, it is my great honor to induct these
> gifted men into the Rock and Roll Hall of Fame.
> Please welcome Bill Medley and Bobby Hatfield,
> the Righteous Brothers.

It was quite a night, a remarkable night. To be with all the music industry and have them tell you what you meant to them, very humbling. Another cool thing that happened that night was that we got to perform "Lovin' Feelin'" with what had to be the closest live reproduction of Phil Spector's "wall of sound" ever. They brought in Paul Shaffer and he assembled an unbelievable orchestra to back us. When we started rehearsing it the day before, I started and then stopped singing in disbelief. It sounded *just* like the record. It was an amazing night, God bless Paul Shaffer—he's like the historian of rock and roll.

> **Paul Shaffer**   I was first introduced to the Righteous Brothers on *Shindig*, which aired on TV in my hometown of Thunder Bay, Ontario. It was explosive—you got to see Bill and Bobby really in their element, soulful and doing this R&B duet thing with its roots in gospel call and response. It was all very magical to me.
>
> At the Hall of Fame induction our aim was to re-create the "wall of sound" and for me it was the realization of a lifetime dream. I had something like thirty guys, and came as close as I could to replicating that brilliant Phil Spector sound. I'd been studying to do that my whole life. I'm still studying that record, even today I continue to hear new things in there. The main thing is the vocals and the singing Bobby and Bill did. I think we came pretty close to a fitting tribute to the most played song in radio history.

Paul is such a great musician and a really funny guy. Recently I was doing a show in Connecticut where Paul lives. He came to the show with Chevy Chase and their wives. At one point in the show

I did an "unplugged" thing—acoustic guitar, drums, vocals, and piano with my daughter McKenna. It leads into a blues medley and I called Paul up to play the B3 organ. As soon as he got to his place he grabbed the mic and said, "Medley just did his unplugged portion of the show—they didn't unplug a fuckin' thing!" The audience laughed but he was right, we really didn't unplug anything. Now I refer to it as my "story-telling" part of the show.

Having Paul, Billy Joel, and so many others celebrate with us at the Hall of Fame induction was a great moment for me, Bobby, and our families. What we didn't know is that it would be the last time we all gathered together to celebrate. The next time we gathered it was for a different reason—the day the Righteous Brothers, as the world knew them, died.

25 | November 5, 2003

We flew into Kalamazoo, Michigan, to start a tour. On the plane I noticed that Bobby looked chalky, his color wasn't good. That night, when we checked into the hotel we decided we'd all have dinner together. I'll never forget it. As I was coming down the escalator Bobby was waiting for me. He stopped me and said, "I'm not feeling well, I'm gonna go to my room and eat there."

I said, "Well, are you OK?" It was strange. He was like a little boy; it was like I was talking to the eleven-year-old boy inside of Bobby who, for that moment, wasn't scared anymore—just sweet little Bobby. He was different, his mannerisms and everything, it was odd.

I said, "You sure?"

He said, "Yeah, I'll see you later Beany."

He'd never called me Beany in my life. He had a nickname for me, "Bean," like beanpole, but never Beany. Those were the last words I ever heard from Bobby's mouth—he went up to his room and died.

I should have known something was wrong. Even the band noticed how unusual it was for Bobby to go to his room at nine o'clock. Sitting at the bar, smoking and drinking and telling jokes was the most fun Bobby had in his life.

The next day the band was already at the Miller Auditorium on the campus of Western Michigan University where we were scheduled to perform. I was getting ready to leave the hotel. Bobby usually went earlier than me, he liked to get settled, smoke a few cigarettes, and have some coffee before the show. I like to show up just before I go on, slap on a little makeup, and walk onstage. Just as I was getting ready to walk out my hotel room door I got a call from Dusty Hanvey, our road manager at the time, saying he couldn't find Bobby. He'd called Bobby's room and knocked on the door but no one answered.

Dusty called security and they noticed it was locked from the inside. I wasn't too concerned because this had happened a few times before when Bobby had gotten so drunk and passed out that we had to break into his hotel room. Actually, that's not true, I was concerned. Every time it had happened in the past I wondered if this would be the final time because Bobby just didn't take care of himself. I was concerned but not surprised. Honestly, I think if God had a conversation with Bobby and asked if he wanted to stay or go Bobby would have said, "Take me." Now, I don't believe he ever would've wanted to leave his wife and kids, but the truth is Bobby Hatfield was never comfortable in his own skin.

The security guard let us in and there was Bobby, lying on the bed with the TV remote in his hand. He was gone. I walked to the bed, bent over, and kissed him on the forehead. "Bobby. Bobby. Bobby." I said as tears welled in my eyes.

I thought, "Jesus, forty years—we went through stuff that nobody in the world could understand but Bobby and me. Now it's really gone. The Righteous Brothers are gone. I don't have the option of knocking on Bobby's door and saying let's go out and be the Righteous Brothers anymore. He's gone."

They called the paramedics but it was way too late. Then we had to call the band and tell them there wasn't going to be a show because Bobby had passed away. That was such a hard thing; it kind of reminded me of when I had to tell Darrin that his mom had passed.

I knew that as soon as it leaked out it would be all over the news so I called Bobby's wife Linda right away. Linda's mom Connie answered and I said, "I need to speak with Linda." She said, "Well, she's taking a nap."

"This is real important, Bobby passed away," I said.

She replied, "I'll have her call you."

"Uh, OK—but immediately."

Within a few minutes Linda called. Unfortunately, Connie didn't tell her Bobby had died. When my phone rang Linda said, "Hey Bill, what's up?"

My heart stopped. I said, "Well, sit down—Bobby passed away."

She said, "No, no, no—I have something to tell him."

While fighting through my own heartbreak I was also racing the clock to let my family and friends know what had happened. I knew the West Coast news reports would hit immediately and say something like "Righteous Brother dies, more in our six o'clock news." I didn't want my family to panic thinking it was me. Even before I had called Linda I phoned everyone else I knew who might help and told them to get over to Bobby's house right away to be with her and the kids. Thankfully, people got there and surrounded them.

Bobby's best friend Jim Owens Bobby and his wife Linda were at our house in La Jolla the weekend before he passed. Everything seemed fine, we had a great time. He called me the following Monday and we talked for about an hour, he told me he was going to Kalamazoo to start a short Midwest tour then heading off to Vegas for a three-week run. We made plans to meet in Vegas.

On Wednesday my phone rang at 4:15, and I remember it vividly, it said Doubletree Hotel on the caller ID. I answered, "Hello?"

"Jimmy, this is Bill."

"How you doin'?" I asked.

"I'm not doing good; we've got a show in forty minutes and Bobby is gone."

"Where'd he go?"

Then Bill gave me the news, "No, he's passed away, he died in his sleep. He's right next to me. I'm standing right here and he's got the TV clicker in his hand."

I lost it. Bill said, "I really need you to be strong for me right now. Get up to Newport Beach to be with Linda when I tell her." My wife and I jumped in the car and got there by the time Bill called her, it was just devastating. I helped Linda pick out the casket and they had a private viewing the night before. I went to the mortuary but I didn't want to see him in the casket. I just sat there. It was tough but I finally did go up and I was glad I did.

It was a shock but it wasn't a surprise to any of us, Bobby was just wrung out. After each show he'd virtually collapse offstage. We had a chair there for him and I'd stay with him until I was sure he was OK.

Looking back I thought about the times I'd told Bobby to get to a doctor because I knew something was wrong. Bobby would say, "OK, do you have one?" He didn't even have a doctor; he never let himself think about it. I should have known that I had to go over to his house and take him by the hand to my doctor. They could have found out that his arteries were blocked and done something to help him.

I went back to my room and they took Bobby to the morgue. The next day Dusty called and told me they had our flight home arranged but I told them to go ahead, I wasn't going to leave without Bobby. I couldn't fathom leaving Bobby in Kalamazoo by himself. God bless him, Michael Gaughan called and said he'd send his private plane but it wasn't big enough to hold the casket so I waited for a commercial flight. When I finally flew home there was a sea of paparazzi waiting for us. In fact, as soon as the news broke in Kalamazoo the paparazzi was all over the hotel lobby waiting to find out what had happened. It really pissed me off that the minute they found out it was a heart attack they just left. They fuckin' just left— like if it wasn't some sensational scandal they weren't interested.

Show business can be so cruel. When we told the promoter in Michigan the show had to be cancelled because Bobby had died he said, "Jesus, what else can go wrong." The band came back to the hotel and we gathered in the restaurant and told funny Bobby stories. It was a heavy day. We were a family. As many ups and downs as Bobby and I had over the years, you can't go onstage for forty years with someone unless you have each other's backs. Bobby and I and the band always had each other's backs.

A month later, when the toxicology report came back and they found there was cocaine in Bobby's system the press was interested again. They ran all kinds of stories about it. The medical examiner's final report acknowledged the cocaine, but pointed to advanced coronary disease as the real cause of death. It read, *In this case, there was already a significant amount of blockage in the coronary arteries.*

None of us knew Bobby had used cocaine, and that may have triggered the heart attack, but the truth is Bobby Hatfield just didn't work at staying alive. My hand to God, I never knew Bobby was using cocaine—I would have done something, maybe left the group. I went on Larry King's show on CNN and *The O'Reilly Factor* on Fox and defended Bobby. He did not die from cocaine; he died because he was in horrible health and never went to see a doctor, period.

I knew something really serious was going on. He was eating like a horse but just couldn't keep any weight on. There was always a huge room service tray with finished malts and hamburgers outside his hotel room door and that didn't fit with the cocaine thing either, guys using cocaine don't eat like that. Bobby was just worn out, how he performed those last few years I'll never know.

I had grown to accept Bobby for who he was. I'm the best Bill Medley in the world and he was the best Bobby Hatfield. Someone once asked me why I didn't help Bobby stop smoking and drinking so he could sing and perform better. I said, "Listen, the one thing Bobby loves to do is go to the bar and smoke and drink—he loves it! He doesn't love to perform, it scares him—it's not a natural thing for him. So, you want me to try to convince Bobby to stop doing what he loves to do, so he can do a better job at something he doesn't like to do? I don't have a prayer of that!"

His memorial service was held at Mariners Church in Irvine, California. I remember driving over there with McKenna, Paula, Jennifer Warnes, and Brad Garrett. Brad asked me, "Bill how can I do this, should I be funny at all?" I told him, "You better be or Bobby will come down and get you." It's what Bobby would have wanted. Brad was enormously funny, I'll always remember one thing he said as he eulogized Bobby, "Five words you'd never hear from Bobby Hatfield—let's call it a night."

Brad Garrett　Bobby and I had a lot of early mornings, Bill was just the opposite. Bill was in bed by eleven, but not Bobby. These were in the days before I stopped drinking—I stopped drinking about sixteen years ago, thank goodness. I was in my twenties but Bobby was in his late forties at the time and I still had trouble staying with him. He loved to gamble and he loved to drink, we'd stay up until 6 a.m. and then go right to the golf course. I'd ask him, "How do you do this?" The boy just loved to play as hard as he worked. Bobby would outlast everybody—the bartenders, the band, me— everyone. We really had some fun.

At the service McKenna told a wonderful story about her "Uncle Bobby," he was one of her favorite people in the world. I told her later how proud I was of her for loving him because she knew Bobby and I had some problems over the years. Jennifer Warnes sang "Amazing Grace"—it was just beautiful. I played piano and sang "Precious Lord," and somehow made it through. I really had to focus on what I was singing because if I focused on Bobby I would have lost it. Most of the service was a blur, I was out to lunch. Connie Stevens and Paul Revere spoke, they were great.

We laid him to rest in Corona del Mar in a beautiful cemetery, but I don't remember much about that either; I was in a daze. A few years ago on Bobby's birthday I visited the gravesite with Nino

Tempo. I was clear-headed then and got a chance to really talk to Bobby. I told him I loved him and missed him and reminisced about the old times. Now, over a decade past that terrible day, I do feel I have closure about it—but I still get wound up when people start talking about the old times. I get pissed off at the situation more than anything; it just didn't have to turn out that way.

I often remember one of the only things Bobby ever said to me that wasn't a joke. We were at my home in Orange County out on my pier at night. The ocean is just beautiful and it feels like a place that's close to God. We were talking about how his younger brother John had passed away and then his older brother Carl, and Bobby looked at me and said, "I don't get it. I don't understand why my brothers are dead and I'm still alive. I'm the one who should be dead."

That was one of maybe three times in our relationship that we had a real guy-to-guy connection. About a year later he passed. I miss Bobby Hatfield. In every concert now I do a tribute to him, I sing "Unchained Melody" while video screens flash pictures of our life together. In that way I keep the Righteous Brothers and Bobby alive in my heart. I can't tell you how glad I am that our last years together were our best years together, not as "stars" but as human beings. I'll tell you this, there will *never* be another Bobby Hatfield.

26 | The Fans

As I get older I think I appreciate the fans who still come to my shows even more. Every time I walk onstage I'm genuinely surprised at the full houses of smiling faces singing along with the hits. For that moment I'm twenty-five again and I think the audiences go there too. We can forget about being mature adults for a while and just have a ball.

After my shows I usually spend an hour or so signing stuff and taking pictures with the fans. They tell me story after story of how the Righteous Brothers music touched their lives; it's very cool and very humbling. The cutest thing about the public is the difference between what the guys and girls say. The men come up and say, "Man, I can't tell you how many times I got laid in the backseat listening to your music." Then the guy's wife comes over and says, "I can't tell you how many romantic evenings we had with your music." It's happened hundreds of times, and if that doesn't show you the difference between men and women, I don't know what does!

I think the most touching stories center on the Vietnam War era. We weren't aware of it at the time but our music was really big for the service men and women in Vietnam. Veterans come up at every show and say, "I can't tell you how you saved our lives over there. Sometimes we'd be going right into battle singing "Lovin' Feelin'" or "Unchained Melody" or "Soul and Inspiration.""

Wow. Guys with no legs would come up and give me and Bobby flags or pins—stuff they had in the war and they're giving it to *us*. Man, if that's all our careers did—God, thank you. Big burly guys still come up to me after my shows and their wives say, "He'll never tell you, but he's your biggest fan—you so helped him through Vietnam." Then I look up at the guy behind her and tears are flowing down his cheeks. It brings show business to a whole other level.

When I'd perform "Unchained Melody" in my Branson shows I'd dedicate it to the veterans. I'd visualize them standing by the ocean and writing the lyrics to their families at home—*Oh, my love, my darling—I hunger for your touch.* When you've got a guy coming up to you with no legs or no arms and giving *you* a flag and thanking *you*—all the bullshit stops.

During Vietnam we performed at a lot of bases for the guys who were just about to ship over and we knew a lot of those guys wouldn't be coming back. We were used to cheers from teenage girls but the roar, I mean *roar*, from these guys was deafening. They were going over to get their asses blown off for us, and they're cheering us? Since that time I've had a special place in my heart for the veterans. A few years ago I performed with my friend Paul Revere at the Rolling Thunder event in Washington, D.C.—it's a big group of motorcycle guys who refuse to forget the veterans, POWs, and MIAs. Something like 900,000 people showed up, Connie Stevens and Nancy Sinatra were there too.

A few years ago McKenna and I, along with Miss America, went to the Bethesda Naval Hospital in Washington, D.C., and met with the returning vets from Iraq. Of course, most of them didn't know me. I'd introduce myself and say, "You can ask your mom and dad or grandparents about me." These kids just broke my heart. They're lying there shot to hell, many of them missing limbs, and all they could talk about was how they'd like to get back to their "brothers" on the front lines.

I started thinking, "Man, whatever I'm bitchin' about, I gotta quit bitchin' about anything." That's the one thing that pisses me off the most about myself; I can't keep how fortunate I am in the front of my brain. The minute I see a homeless person or a veteran it stays in my brain for about an hour, then I start complaining about something stupid—like a meal in a restaurant. It infuriates me that I'm not always grateful. It's the thing I'm least proud of in my life; I'm working on it.

From the very beginning I've been floored by the way the Righteous Brothers' fans have stuck with us, through all the ups and downs, for two generations. As I said in the introduction to the book, there was nothing about the Righteous Brothers that should have worked. Years ago I came up with a theory—the impossible is more probable than the obvious. What I mean is this: the impossible is Bob Dylan. The obvious is some guy that sounds like Elvis, looks like Elvis, and wants to be Elvis. I mean, if you had Bob Dylan on *American Idol* today he probably wouldn't even get through the first round. Being unique is what I think gets and keeps the public's attention.

There was something about the chemistry between Bobby, me, and the music that just worked, even though it didn't make sense. We were two clean-cut white kids from Orange County, California, who sounded black. Maybe it was because we didn't scare the white kids, we were kind of like the Elvis Presley of the "blue-eyed soul" thing. I'm not comparing us to Elvis, he was a phenomenon—

but because we dressed nice and didn't look rough, we somehow made R&B music palatable for white America. Some of the other white R&B artists from that era looked and acted really tough, and I don't think people were ready for that.

Along those lines, our exposure on *Shindig* was just perfect. Our hair was neatly combed and we wore these bitchin' matched suits—in some way that made all the soulful singing and sweat-soaked energy OK. People often hear with their eyes and we didn't scare off the moms and dads, so they let their kids watch.

I think another thing that helped our fans stick with us was that we weren't trying to be like anyone else. I've never stolen a vocal "lick" in my life. Sure, I've been influenced by the Ray Charles, Bobby Blue Bland, Little Richard, and B. B. King records I poured into my ears as a kid, but I never consciously stole a certain lick or phrasing from them. Whatever's in my heart and head at the time, that's what comes out. I think people are really attracted to something they don't totally "get" at first, but they know they love it. Like, "Wow, who are these guys and why do I like them?" I think Bobby had the same unique thing going; the fans loved him because he was Bobby, not a copy of someone else.

Bobby's best friend Jim Owens   One thing Bobby just loved about being a Righteous Brother was the fans. Bill always wanted to perform more than Bobby did; Bobby liked to take it easy. Every year he'd tell me he thought this was going to be his last year but he kept coming back for the fans—he loved them. I was with him a lot and people would always come up and tell him how much the Righteous Brothers' music meant to them.

He always had something funny to say back to make
them feel at ease. I'll never forget, one night in Vegas
a couple approached him and said, "Our first child
was conceived listening to 'Unchained Melody.'
Without missing a beat Bobby turned to them with
a deadpan face and said, "Gee, I wish I'd been there!"

People always ask how I keep singing the same hit songs over and over again. I tell them the minute I start I go right back to where I was then, and I get a kick out of watching them go back too. They tell me that I, the Righteous Brothers, or a certain song was a marker in their life—what an honor.

Once when I did a gospel album, I thought, "If this touches just one person it's worth it." I've had notes slid under my door on the road about how a song from that album got someone through a rough time. I can't tell you how good that feels.

The truth is I feel loved, not admired—that's a real different deal to me. Now, at seventy-three, I can take my daily walk and people say, "Hi Bill." After about the third time they say, "Hey, can I talk to you for a minute? I know who you are and I don't wanna bother you, but I've heard enough about you," etc. It's real person-to-person stuff, no celebrity bullshit. It's different from them just liking what I do or did.

It's hard for me to think of the people who attend my shows now as *fans*, I consider them *friends*. If true wealth is counted by the friends you have who stick with you through the years, I'm probably the richest man alive. To anyone who has ever bought a Righteous Brothers or Bill Medley record (CD or digital file now, I guess) or come to a show, thank you so much. You gave me much more than I ever gave you.

27 | Beyond Bobby

In the years since Bobby passed I've never stopped performing. In fact, I probably went back way too soon. In 2001 and 2002, before Bobby died, I'd done a Christmas tour without him called *Colors of Christmas*. It featured mostly black artists like Peabo Bryson, Marilyn McCoo, and Roberta Flack. I was really the only white guy invited, that made me feel kind of special and the crowds were fantastic. In addition to the Christmas music I'd do my hits and I'd have the audience sing along and do Bobby's parts. The black audiences were always great with that; they jumped right in.

One night in Detroit Aretha Franklin was sitting right in the front row. Of course everybody knew she was there, she's the Queen of Soul and she'd grown up in Detroit, it was her town. When I started doing "Lovin' Feelin'" the crowd didn't sing along, they bowed to the Queen. From her seat in the front row, without a microphone, she nailed Bobby's parts like nothing I'd ever heard. It was a once-in-a-lifetime moment.

I had a lot of fun doing *Colors of Christmas* in 2001 and 2002 and after Bobby passed away in November of 2003 they asked if I'd do it again in December. Apparently, someone had dropped out and they needed a fill-in for a few dates.

Without thinking I said, "Yeah, sure." The first date was at the Cerritos Center for the Performing Arts in Southern California, and the moment I hit the stage I thought, "Oh man, I do not belong up here." It was like walking into a fog, I just felt lost. I didn't realize how drained I was and how much I'd been affected by Bobby's death. Not only was it weird for me, it was weird for the audience too, they sensed something was off. I stumbled my way through the show and told the producers I couldn't do the rest of the dates. That was my first clue that losing Bobby had taken more out of me than I'd thought. I'd performed so much on my own that I never expected it to be a problem, but it was. It was just too soon.

I still had the big ten-piece Righteous Brothers band and we had contracts to fulfill; I wanted to keep them working if I could. I decided we'd go out as a Righteous Brothers show and do something like a tribute to Bobby. It was a really stupid thing to do. I should have taken a year or two off. I wasn't ready for it. What I came to realize was that when Bobby passed away the Righteous Brothers died, and I was part of the Righteous Brothers. A part of me died with Bobby Hatfield and going out with *our* band and basically doing *our* show didn't work.

The audiences were very sweet and they reacted fine, but it was awkward. It was like they were there to pay their respects to Bobby and that made it a tough environment to perform in. It was almost too solemn. If I'd gone out as Bill Medley with my own band I would have been much better mentally and physically—and it would have been a better show. It was way too soon for everyone. In hindsight I wish I'd just rested and processed what had happened.

In the year after Bobby passed, David Cohen was putting together a deal for me in Branson, which at the time was booming as a growing vacation destination. My old business partner from The Hop, Bob Copeland, was in Branson producing an oldies show and one of his friends was building a great new venue, the Dick Clark American Bandstand Theater. I don't think Dick was much involved other than lending his name to it because he'd had a stroke and was really struggling with his health at that time.

Bob's friend asked him for advice, and Bob told him to get in touch with me because I knew how to produce the kinds of shows that would work in a place like that. David made the deal and I called Paul Revere and told him, "I have an opportunity to go to Branson, and I probably wouldn't do it, but it's called the Dick Clark American Bandstand Theater and we're rock & roll, we should do it together." My son Darrin was singing lead for Paul Revere and the Raiders at the time and Paul's band backed me up so it was a neat little package. It also gave me tons of time with my son, which was great.

The theater itself is great, they did it right. It has a themed restaurant, gift shop, beautiful décor, and a really cool, state-of-the-art showroom. It was just a perfect fit, I'd been on *American Bandstand* more times than I can remember, and Paul Revere also had a great connection with Dick Clark ever since Dick's *Where the Action Is* TV show premiered in 1965 with Paul and the Raiders as the regular house band.

The first year we did steady increasing business, right on target. The following year we really started to take off. I loved it because Paul is a close friend and literally one of the funniest guys I know. The audiences were just terrific, and by the end of the second year we were doing near sellout business every night. We'd do two weeks on and then two weeks off. For our off weeks they built a really fun package show with Bobby Vee, Fabian, Brian Hyland, Chris Montez, and a great little band that featured two of Bobby Vee's kids. It was different from our show, a great package of singers and songs, one right after another—they were super-entertaining.

Everything was going great until the economy tanked. When the economy took a dump in 2008 that poor little town just crashed, as did Vegas, and most of the other entertainment spots around the country. Fabian, Bobby Vee, and the guys from that show figured it out right away and decided to leave. Paul and I stuck it out and tried to think of a way to make it work. In 2009 we moved the show over to Andy Williams' Moon River Theatre, but that wasn't much help.

I started wondering if I was getting a little old to be working so hard, but moving the show over to Andy's place proved to be a real inspiration for me. I'd known him for many years; we'd been guests on his TV show in the 1960s when he was really popular. One day the theater manager approached me and said, "Andy wants to see you in his office." I felt kind of like I was getting called to the principal's office, all of a sudden I was fifteen years old again. When I got there Andy said, "Hi, Billy." He always called me Billy for some reason. He continued, "I see that you're wearing that in-ear monitor. I just bought some from the Osmonds and wondered if you'd mind working with me a bit on how to use them. I don't know anything about them, would you help me?"

"Sure," I said. I showed him how I only use them in one ear because with both in I feel too confined, like in a recording studio. With just one side in I can still hear the audience and the instruments with my other ear. We walked through it and he ended up loving them. I told him another benefit is that you sing about 25 percent softer when using them so you save your voice; he really liked that.

After I was done it dawned on me—here's this guy who's eighty-two years old and he's still trying to learn and be as good as he can for himself and the audience. I thought that was so remarkable. Most people get to a certain age and just say, "Well, that's how I do it." Even though he was a legend and had one of the greatest voices in the world, he was always trying to make his voice better and improve his show. Every young act in the country should take a piece of that history and learn that lesson.

As much as I loved working with Andy and being at his theater, the downturn in the economy eventually forced us to leave. I was really bummed because for me Branson was paradise. Just being there with Darrin was great because when he was born I'd just had a hit with "Lovin' Feelin'" and that cheated us out of a lot of time together. McKenna also established herself there, so I got to spend a ton of time with her too. How it happened was, when she was nineteen she came for a visit and did "Time of My Life" with me live onstage—just a one-time thing. The owners of the theater fell in love with her and made her an offer she couldn't refuse, so she stayed. It was funny. Here's this little girl raised on the ocean in Newport Beach and now they have her staying at the Ramada Inn next door to the theater for two years. She loved it; she did an afternoon oldies show and also sang with Les Brown, Jr., doing big band stuff—then worked with me at Dick Clark's. She was making an incredible living for a young girl. I used to tell people she was the hardest working nineteen year old in the world, she had three jobs! She even designed and built her own four-bedroom house—how many young people can do that? Paula and I are super-proud of her.

I was in heaven. Not only was I there with my son, my daughter, and Paula—I got to build my dream house. It was my "bucket list" home and I literally could have walked to work—it was that close. I'd leave my house at 7:30, be onstage by 8:00, be done and sign autographs and talk with the fans until maybe 10:30, and then go home for dinner. Six nights a week—that was a dream. I loved the town too. I'd tell Darrin, "I feel like I'm living in Knott's Berry Farm, everyone is so sweet and nice."

Finally Paul and I figured out the only chance we had to stay in Branson was for us to split up. He stayed at Andy Williams' theater and I went down the street to another venue called the Starlite. The management and theater were great, but from a financial perspective it just didn't work. Many of those Branson showrooms have closed in the past few years, although the Dick Clark Theater is hanging on with one of those celebrity impersonator shows—it's really good. These days I only go there to visit my house, but I *love* that house. I try to spend two or three months there every year.

Let me tell you about it. As I said, it was one of my "bucket list" things to get out of my system. It sits on twenty acres, we built a pond on it and it has a stream running through it. In the fall it looks like God came along and painted the joint, it's just beautiful. The main house has 5,000 square feet and there's a cute little cabin on the property we use as a guesthouse. It's something I hope my grandkids enjoy with their families long after I'm gone. I knew exactly what I wanted but, like The Hop, Paula was the one who really made it come to life.

Paula Medley Building that house was too much fun for words. He kept making it bigger and bigger. I'm like, "Bill, the pond is going to cost a hundred thousand dollars!" He'd say, "Yeah, but this is what I want to create." Bill drew out the floor plans and

I decorated it. I know sometimes people say building a house can cause marital problems but in our case it was like, "Wow, we're painting this picture together." We've never had more fun.

Because our tastes are so similar, we decided it would be like a Jackson Hole ski lodge. I've never seen Bill more proud than when people would come over and he'd give them the tour. Our first Thanksgiving there was probably the best Thanksgiving we've ever had. It was so social, everybody was cooking everywhere—the cabin, the bunkhouse, and the main kitchen. Then we all came together upstairs for the meal, it was great.

The thing about that house is it's probably the biggest financial mistake of our lives. But when we look back and think, it's probably the most fun five years we've had. Money isn't everything.

After Branson dried up I went back to the road again and was reminded of how different it is. In Branson the "Strip" is full of shows and a lot of the visitors are vacationers, just cramming in one show after another. They come in on buses and their days are planned out. A lot of them are older. I used to joke, "The buses are filled with old people and their parents." By the time it was dark they'd be worn out. Sometimes they'd fall asleep in the front row—not good for a performer's ego.

When I'm on the road it's different. The people who come to my shows are coming to see Bill Medley. I have their attention from the start. The one-nighters are a bit harder because of the travel, but the crowds are just great. Sometimes I walk out onstage and get a standing ovation for just being there. Maybe they're excited that I can still walk!

When I was young, Las Vegas, Reno, and Lake Tahoe were the big stops for entertainers. Now there are small casinos all over the country and that's opened up a lot of work for musicians. The Native American casinos have become what used to be the lounges in Vegas. You won't find a big lounge anywhere in Vegas anymore, so working one-nighters at the casinos brings back a lot of that old Vegas lounge fun and energy.

Part of the fun I've had in the last ten years or so is performing with my band. Not only are they great musicians, they're great friends. Larry Hanson goes way back with me, to The Hop shows in the 1980s. When I was the opening act for Alabama he was in my band. We finished the tour and they asked if they could borrow him—they didn't give him back for eighteen years. He's a great guitar and keyboard player and blows a mean saxophone too. Larry's a solid, wonderful family guy.

Bob Gulley was another guy who was with me for years. I'd used him at Medley's restaurant before it became The Hop with his band the Exploding Pintos. After Medley's closed, Paula and I were driving up to Big Bear and I was thinking about opening The Hop and doing the *Rock Around the Clock* show. I saw a sign on a little roadside place on the way that said "Tonight—Bob Gulley!" We went inside and Bob, Tim Lee, and Bobby Cruz were playing there. I began to tell them about my idea for The Hop show and they thought it was great, they all agreed to appear in it right then and there.

It's funny, Bob Gulley has one of the best voices I've ever heard, but I'd have to push him to do big dramatic ballads in the show. Real emotional stuff like the Platters' "Smoke Gets in Your Eyes" and "My Prayer." He complained about it every time, but after he'd sing them the audience would go nuts. He'd pass me and say, "Alright, you were right again." Years later Bob went to Branson and won Male Vocalist of the Year honors there. Then he just left. I don't think Branson was something he wanted to do.

Another guy who goes way back with me is Tim Lee, my current road manager and bandleader. Tim's a great piano player and singer. I count on him to make sure everything's right when we're on the road so I can put all my energy into the show. Tim's a good, good friend.

> **Tim Lee** Bill was always a hometown boy. After all his success he ended up living in Orange County, where he grew up. He's comfortable there and that's where his family and friends are. I think that's how he is with the band too; we're all comfortable with each other. There are certainly some hotshot players he could have gotten, but they wouldn't have had the stability and sense of family we have. When you're living in close quarters on a bus the ability to get along is a big plus.
>
> One thing I learned early on with Bill is that he wants it right, every time. When I first started working with him we were in Lake Tahoe and sometimes at the really late show there would be maybe ten people in the audience. I'd be really tired and mentally done for the night and then I'd see Bill going 110 percent. I began thinking, "I better step up." No excuses with Bill. When you're on stage you deliver everything you've got. That really struck me early on in our relationship.

A couple of other guys I should mention are Jamie Browning and Gabe Rabben. Jamie is another Orange County guy who's worked with me on and off for years. He's a terrific guitar player, singer, and songwriter. Sometimes I do a three-part a capella thing with Jamie and McKenna that just knocks the audiences out.

Most of my current band are guys who are within about a twenty-year range of me—in other words we're all old. That is except Gabe. He's like the adopted son of our group. I think he started with me when he was about twenty-one and now he's been with me a few years. Pretty soon he might be too famous to be my drummer. He writes songs with McKenna and he's got a group called Friends of Lola. I think they're going to be a big hit.

It's funny, I'm on the back side of seventy and things are not only going strong, I'm getting busier. Last November I appeared in England for the first time at Wembley Arena. Can you believe that with all the success and following the Righteous Brothers had in England we never appeared there? Not one concert. We went there to promote our records, did tons of TV shows and interviews, but never a concert. Wembley Arena, how cool is that? It was a great experience. I went over a couple of months early to promote the concert, and as soon as my plane landed the promoters whisked me off to a giant soccer field outside of London. When I got there I discovered why—the Nottingham Forest professional soccer team blasts "Lovin' Feelin'" in their stadium every time they score a goal. They walked me out on the field and I led the enthusiastic crowd of something like 25,000 pumped-up sports fans through the song. What a rush! You can see a few different videos of it on YouTube.

Another cool thing happened when I went to England to promote that concert. They asked if I had any new recordings to give to their radio and TV stations, and I told them I did a blues album, called *Your Heart to Mine*, which I never released. I did it more for my own sake than for commercial success; it's a tribute to many of the black artists who influenced me—Ray Charles, Bobby Blue Bland, B.B. King, Sam Cooke, and the like. I never even let a record company hear it; I just needed to get it off my chest.

When it arrived in England the radio stations started playing it and people just loved it. I ended up sending it to Fuel Records in Los Angeles and they loved it too. They released it in April of 2014. It's the first new album I've released since 2007, and if you really want to know what music inspires me you'll find it there. I included an original song, "This Will Be the Last Time," which I wrote especially for this project. When I do it in my live show it gets a great response. It's my heartfelt thanks to the singers I love so much. I can always tell if a song is working when I sing it live, either it moves the audience or it doesn't. Making records is great, but nothing does it for me like performing for a live audience.

Whether it's an arena like Wembley, an arts center in Florida, or a casino in Iowa, I still love to perform—maybe more than ever. Of course, part of the magic for me is that my kids are doing well and I adore my wife. Without my friends and family it wouldn't mean much at all. Performing is the icing, my family and friends are the cake.

28 | Kid Stuff

After Karen passed away, raising Darrin as a single parent really forced me to grow up. Even though I had a lot of help from friends like Connie Stevens and many others, I still had to be a dad. It was new for me and I didn't always get it right, but one thing I wanted Darrin to know was that he could count on me. As much as it was in my control, I wasn't going to bail on him—ever.

> **Darrin Medley** I've done a lot of things in my life, I've made mistakes for sure, but the one thing I really pride myself on is that I'm a good parent— and I learned that from my dad. I don't do anything better than loving my children, I learned that from him.
>
> When I was thirteen years old I came home with a bad report card and he got very frustrated and over-reacted, like many parents do, and grounded me until the next report card came out. I had to come straight home from school

every day and there was no fun on the weekends. I was very upset about it; I thought it was way too severe and unfair.

The next day dad came to me and said, "I want you to know I over-reacted. The punishment I gave you was too harsh. I was angry, but you're gonna live it out and go through with it, because I don't ever want you to doubt my word."

At the time I thought that was crazy, but it ended up being the best life lesson I ever got from him, because I knew when my dad said something it was for real. That's one thing I've taken forward with my kids. It creates amazing kids because they know they can count on you. What I really want people to know about Bill Medley is that my dad taught me what it means to be a good father.

In some ways Darrin was a lot like me as a teenager, he loved riding motorcycles. Once when I was in a recording studio in Costa Mesa, I got a call that Darrin had been in a bad wreck. He was a great motocross rider and he was competing at a big event in the Anaheim Stadium. He'd taken a huge jump and fell when he landed. That wasn't the bad part though. The guy right behind him landed on him and broke Darrin's back.

Paula met me at the studio and we rushed to the hospital. His brother Damien was already there—they were always together, competing with each other, spurring each other on to do crazier and crazier things. Damien had been videotaping Darrin's race, and by the time we got to the hospital they already had the camera hooked up to the TV in his room and were watching the crash.

He was showing me the whole thing in slow motion and I'm like, "Jeez, I don't wanna see that!" The guy's motorcycle had crushed one of Darrin's vertebrae; as it turned out he was less than a quarter-inch away from never walking again.

Paula kind of took over and they moved him to another hospital. They had to do an eight-hour operation. After the surgery I walked into his room and asked, "Do you know how lucky you are? The doc told me you were just a smidgeon away from being in a wheelchair the rest of your life!"

> **Darrin Medley**   I'm very lucky to be walking.
> My fracture was what is called a "burst" fracture. My
> doctor described it as being like what happens when
> you hit a walnut with a hammer. The vertebrae
> bursts and pieces of the broken spine go into the
> spinal cord. He said I was extremely fortunate that
> it didn't sever my spinal cord completely.

Every time I see Darrin I thank God for the good things that have come from the pain in his life. He's not just a success in business (his company employs over three hundred people), he's a success as a man. What more could a dad ask for from his son?

Darrin was in his early twenties and already a father himself when McKenna was born. In that sense they're from two different generations. The Bill Medley who raised Darrin and the Bill Medley who raised McKenna were different guys as well. I don't know how much wiser I was, but I was older and at a different point in my career and life with McKenna.

One thing that was different for McKenna was that she had a reasonably stable home. Even though I still traveled a lot, she had her mom there, and her life as a kid was fairly normal, if there is such a thing.

McKenna Medley People ask me all the time what it's like to be Bill Medley's daughter. To me it was very normal because I didn't know anything else. My dad's a pretty grounded guy.

I have felt some pressure because I'm a singer and for a long time people expected me not to be good when they heard I was performing with him. Like, "Oh man, now we have to sit through this." I understand that because there are other entertainers out there who push their kids in front of audiences when maybe they shouldn't. That's always motivated me to work harder and get better because I know people's expectations are high. I never wanted to come out just because it's a "cute" bit. Thankfully I got my dad's genes and it's worked out pretty well.

I started singing with dad when I was five or six. I liked it but I was extremely shy. Being onstage actually helped because, for some reason, I've always been more comfortable onstage than offstage.

Even though McKenna grew up with two loving parents and certain advantages, her life hasn't been a fairy tale. That darn social anxiety thing that my family wrestles with and the automatic scrutiny of being Bill Medley's daughter have caused some painful seasons in her young life.

McKenna   I left high school to do home studies
my last two years, partly because I was beginning
to travel to perform, but mostly because I just
couldn't handle being at school. I had a few friends
but they were older and when they graduated
I was traumatized by the idea of going back.
Sometimes I'd have my lunch in the bathroom
stall. Even in elementary school I went through
some tough, bad times. I was awkward and
overweight. I went to a private school in Newport
Beach where everyone was expected to look and
act a certain way. I was the opposite of what
most considered "cool."

Even my political views didn't fit. When my dad
got to sing at Bill Clinton's college reunion at the
White House we all got to go. I remember thinking,
"How many people get to stand in the Oval Office,
let alone meet the president?" When I came back
to school some of the other kids were mad and
disgusted with me because I met President Clinton
and he was a Democrat. This is in fifth grade! They'd
say stuff like, "My parents said if they saw Clinton
on the other side of the street they wouldn't even
walk over to say hello."

Being overweight as a kid didn't help my anxiety
either. When I ended up losing the weight I felt
more confident, like I could finally shed this thing
that was holding me down. Another thing that
really helped was that when I moved to Branson I
was surrounded by people who loved and supported

me unconditionally, no matter what. That's when
I started to become comfortable in my own skin,
people accepted me for who I was. I wasn't trying
to be whatever other people liked.

Branson gave me the chance to grow, working
with people who weren't my dad. I did an afternoon
show with amazing artists like Dave Somerville
of the Diamonds, Shirley Alston Reeves and the
Shirelles, the Crickets—lots of seasoned performers.
I've done some country stuff too; I sang at the
National Finals Rodeo recently. I've also gotten to
sing all those great big band songs from the 1940s
with Les Brown and His Band of Renown, led by
Les Brown, Jr.—I love that music.

Paula and I couldn't be more proud of McKenna. She's worked
hard at her craft and continues to. She's been vocalist of the year in
Branson and *417 Magazine* recently named her one of the Midwest's
ten most beautiful women. She's recording a new album in Nashville
as I write this book and it's really good. I love working with her, and
her "Uncle Bobby" would be so proud that she often sings his parts
in our shows.

Even when she was really young McKenna showed an interest in
singing. When she was like two or three years old she started singing
along with TV commercials and Paula would say, "Bill, do you hear
that? Do you think she has a voice?" By the time she'd reached fourteen she was opening in Vegas for the Smothers Brothers and
Frankie Avalon. We're so grateful to our friend Michael Gaughan for
giving her the chance. The audiences liked her so much that he
decided to use her as a headliner at his Suncoast Hotel and Casino.

At age fifteen, McKenna tied Wayne Newton's record for being the youngest headline act in Vegas—ever! It was a really exciting time for all of us, her shows sold out in two days; they even had to add an extra performance.

Being McKenna's dad forced me to think a lot about what it means to be a father to a daughter. I want to share something with all the fathers of daughters; it's a lesson I learned in high school.

I was going with this pretty little girl, Joanne, at Santa Ana High. It was the typical "wrong side of the tracks" thing—she was from the affluent north-end of town and I was the south-end, motorcycle and Levis guy. The teacher made her responsible for me getting my homework done, kind of a tutor thing.

We started dating. I really liked her and was very respectful. I never tried any physical stuff at all, even though we dated quite a while. Her father was an eye doctor, and one day he called and had me make an appointment with him. When I went in he had a little piece of paper in front of him and said, "I'm concerned about you and Joanne."

"Well, OK," I said.

He put two names on the paper, Bill Medley on one side and John Doe on the other. Then he started to write down our assets and liabilities.

"Let's see," he said. "John Doe doesn't smoke, Bill Medley does. John Doe doesn't drink, Bill Medley drinks beer. John Doe graduated from high school and is going to college, Bill Medley dropped out of high school." He went on and on.

By the time he got finished I started thinking, "I'd like to meet this fuckin' John Doe guy, he sounds like a pretty good guy!"

He continued, "I'm afraid you and Joanne are going to elope and I want you to not see my daughter anymore."

I'm a pretty logical guy. After looking at his list I said, "Well, you're probably right. I don't know if you're gonna find John Doe, but Medley's probably headed into a mountain." I left his office and broke up with Joanne. I never told her about the meeting with her dad. Maybe if she reads this she'll finally know.

After we broke up she started dating another singer, not a rock rebel like me, a swing music guy with a lot more polish. I'm sure her dad was far more pleased with her choice. That is until she got pregnant and they "had" to get married. Jeez, I'd never even tried to get to second base with her. It turned out the guy was an alcoholic and they soon got a divorce. By that time I was already a millionaire. The moral of the story is this: I guess you can't judge a book by its cover.

Now, I don't think her dad was wrong for trying to protect his daughter—on paper everything he said made sense, and maybe I wasn't the guy for Joanne. I just wish he'd gotten to know me better before he made up his mind. As much as I've been protective of McKenna, I've tried to let her make her own decisions about dating as she's grown. I advised her just enough to keep her safe, but I wanted her to learn how to figure it out. I think it's important for parents to help their kids learn to make good choices; you can't always do it for them.

While I'm on my soapbox, let me share a few other philosophical thoughts about what really drives me as a person and as a performer. I've spent a lot of my life figuring out what makes me tick—it's not all fun stuff, but it's who I am.

29 | In My Head and Heart

When I hit puberty and my nervous twitches started to develop I began to fear being judged. I decided I was going to be such a tough guy—or such a something—that no one would judge me. As I shared earlier, I discovered that the best way to deal with teasing or a bully was to punch them in the mouth. Nobody wants to fight, at least not kids; they rely on their tough talk as much as they can. I'm certainly not telling kids to go punch each other, but I found out at an early age that if I looked tough, acted tough, and wasn't afraid to throw that first punch people would leave me alone. The bullies would go screw with someone who wouldn't fight back.

Of course it helped that my best friend in junior high was Billy Shiffer. He was a fully grown man in the seventh grade. He put the word out that if you made fun of Medley you were gonna have to deal with him. He was the sweetest guy in the world but nobody dared make fun of me when he was around.

Still, because of the twitches and all the stuff at home with my dad, I was deeply insecure. Somehow that insecurity fueled my desire to perform. I still get hurt really easily; I guess every artist in the world has that insecurity thing going on in one way or another.

Maybe some of it's in my DNA. My brother Leon had the same nerve problems as I did. He was brilliant, an electrical engineer who worked on a lot of the NASA space program stuff when we were going to the moon. After completing college and working a couple years he had a "nervous breakdown" and couldn't get out of bed for three months. He called me and said, "Bill, I don't know what I'm going to do." His wife, an Italian beauty named Rosalie Pitino, had worked to put him through college and now he couldn't take the pressure of working as an engineer. I said, "Well, a friend of mine is selling his pool cleaning business, I can help you buy that." He told me he'd call me back after talking with Rosa. Ten minutes later he called back, "I wanna buy the pool route." I was surprised, but kind of relieved. I knew going back to his engineer job wasn't going to work; if anybody understood his nerve problem it was me. I lent him six thousand dollars to buy the pool business and, even though I really didn't care if I got the money back, Rosalie didn't breathe until they'd paid me in full. He cleaned pools until he passed away a couple years ago—he was my hero.

I tell that story to say that, for whatever reason, anxiety runs in my family and has always been a part of my life. The interesting thing is that it worked for me in the music. The insecurity, the anger, the rebellion—it all comes out in my singing. Unfortunately it also made me become a control freak for many years. I was trying to prevent bad things from happening by controlling everything, and it didn't work. I think that contributed to some of the problems Bobby and I had.

When I sing I'm really not aware of what I'm doing. Sometimes after a song people will ask me, "Where did that come from?" It's like they can feel what's going on inside of me, maybe that's why I like the blues so much. When I get in that place I don't think, it just comes out; I've always been that way. When we first started in Vegas Sammy Davis, Jr., once approached me in the steam room at the Sands with a notepad and pencil in hand. He said, "How do you do it?" I was confused; this was Sammy Davis, one of the greatest entertainers who ever lived. He continued, "When you sing you don't think, how do you do it?" I guess the honest answer is, "I don't know." When I'm singing I'm mentally gone. If I had to think about what I was going to do it wouldn't work for me. I suppose I subconsciously draw on whatever is happening deep in my heart and soul at that moment.

Let me answer Sammy's question this way—I think the music goes from my heart to my voice and doesn't make a stop at my brain. I try to sing from who I am, period. For example, nothing turns me on more than to sing a sad country ballad. If I could do ten of those in every show I would. Like my Ray Charles tribute—"Born to Lose," "You Don't Know Me," and then "I Can't Stop Loving You." Are you kidding me? That lyric—*Born to lose, I've lived my life in vain. All my dreams have only brought me pain. All my life, I've always been so blue. Born to lose, and now I'm losin' you.* That's me man. I was born to lose and I didn't. I know that guy.

To me, country ballads are the white man's blues. I think that's why Ray Charles did that great country album, with strings and a whole orchestra. Those songs tell such great stories. Every time I hear that album I envision a big Presbyterian choir with one little black kid right in the middle of it. I do some country music in every show— I think rock & roll is really a mix of blues, gospel, and country.

These days I think most of my anger is gone, but my wear-it-on-my-sleeve emotions have never left. I well up inside when I do certain songs, especially the soft, simple songs. I don't shout it out like I did once, the anger-driven shouting, but I can still tap into a deep sadness. I don't really know if it's sadness about things from the past, today, or whatever—but it comes out musically and it's almost like medicine for me. As much as in any time of my life, my emotions still drive my singing.

Even though people talk about what a unique voice I have, I've never considered myself a singer. Frank Sinatra and Glen Campbell, those guys are singers. I'm a storyteller. My pain and loneliness invades the music and, coming from this voice God gave me, it seems to work. Maybe that's why I've gotten so many movie and TV theme song gigs; I can tell a story when I sing.

Sometimes I connect with the lyric of a song and sometimes it's just the melody that grabs me. Singing a sad, simple lyric with a sad, simple melody is what I'm really drawn to. When I find a song that comes naturally, one that I don't have to think about, then I can just let it come from my soul. I never consciously think about what I'm going to do vocally, that would ruin it for me. I always try to stay true to the melody, at least for the first verse and chorus. I think it's a mistake to improvise too much; I want to show the song off the way it was written. If I have a vocal technique it's to leave my brain somewhere else and just sing from the heart.

The older I get the more I believe that telling the story is more important than the singing. As talented as the young singers are on all the TV competition shows, sometimes I think they over-sing the songs. That can get in the way of the story. I mean, *Georgia, Georgia. No peace I find. Just an old sweet song keeps Georgia on my mind.* I have no need to help that lyric and melody with some crazy vocal lick, it's a better story as it is. Songwriter Barry Mann once said, "If you want to write a great song for Bill, give him a lot of space so he can say something really good, and then they can think about it."

I learned that giving a song "space," as Barry said, gives the audience time to take it in, to really get involved. Perhaps the master of getting audiences involved was Louis Prima. If you really want to know where I got 90 percent of my knowledge about how to move a live audience, you have to know who Louis Prima was. Louis and his wife Gia Maione were tearing up the lounges in Vegas when Bobby and I first landed there in 1965. Talk about energy—Sam Butera wailing on the sax and the rest of Louis' band were beyond good. They didn't perform *for* you, they performed *to* you and went out and *grabbed* you. They always made the audience part of the show. When Sam would take a sax solo, Louis would stand at his side and cheer him on, "Go, man, go!" It really gave me a direction of how to perform. As great as they were, Frank Sinatra didn't do that; Dean Martin didn't do that.

One time I took a page out of the Prima/Butera book and told my guitar player Barry Rillera to get the longest cord he could find— this was way before the days of wireless connections—and I had him come out in front where I was standing and take a solo. I'd be yelling and encouraging him to let it go and, sure enough, the audience would come right along for the ride. In that day nobody could play guitar like Barry. Jimi Hendrix even said, "The Righteous Brothers have a guitar player that's way ahead of his time." Barry was my Sam Butera.

I became great friends with Sam over time and in his later years he'd work in the lounge at the Orleans when we were in the main room. I'd go see him a lot but I felt kind of bad because he was really showing his age, he was in his late seventies by then. The crazy thing was, even though he could hardly walk, once he got on that stage he'd play and sing like he was nineteen years old. Sam would light the place up, people loved him until the day he stopped performing, about six months before he passed away in 2009 at the age of eighty-one. I owe a lot to Sam and Louis. There's something about those Italians from New Orleans—so much soul, so much passion in everything they did onstage.

Passion, it's what separates a singer from an entertainer. I hope I have passion for my music, my family, and my friends until they start shoveling dirt on my face. I don't work as much as I did when I was twenty-five, but I still love it when I do. Now they've started giving me all sorts of trophies and stuff. They named my high school auditorium after me and finally gave me my diploma. I'm no longer a "drop-out" and I can't wait to tell Hatfield in the hereafter!

Every time I go onstage it's like a first date. I put on my best clothes, shave, and get as handsome as I can. Then I say the cutest things I know to say and I become the very best Bill Medley I can be, because I want to win my date over. My audience is the date I want to impress, every time. I think that's part of what keeps me young, I'm always looking ahead to my next first date—how cool is that?

30 | **Last Call**

People ask me all the time what I think of music today. There are a lot of really talented singers out there; Bruno Mars and Maroon 5 are great. I also love the way John Mayer sings and writes. He's a terrific guitar player too. I love Mumford and Sons—man, that bluegrass harmony just kills me. Zac Brown Band and the Band Perry are two more of my favorites—they have such great energy and Kimberly Perry is as cute as a button. Maybe my absolute favorite is Martina McBride. McKenna reminds me a lot of her with that big voice.

Young people often ask me how to break into the music business, and I almost don't know what to tell them anymore. It's such a different day and time from when I was coming up, everything's on computers today. You can't really walk into a store and buy a record or ask a radio DJ to play your song, those days are gone forever. Even with my own daughter McKenna, who's won all kinds of awards in Branson for Vocalist of the Year, I hardly have a clue what to tell her—and I've been in the music business all my life. Thankfully, she really likes country and country rock; there's still a little life left for new artists in country music.

I guess my best advice is to find a great song that fits your voice, scrape together a few nickels to record it, and put it on the Internet. Unfortunately, with all of today's TV competition shows and social media exposure, young people hardly have a chance to learn their craft before they're shoved into the national spotlight. Even for those who are ready, it's hard to remember the really good performers because there are so many shows.

One great example is my close friend Michael Grimm, who won the fifth season of NBC-TV's *America's Got Talent*. Michael is a great singer and guitar player who, prior to entering that competition, played guitar and sang in my band. They didn't talk about that a lot on the show. I think his being a seasoned professional made it feel a bit unfair to the other contestants—especially in the finals, where his co-finalist was little Jackie Evancho, who was just ten at the time. Michael went on to win the million-dollar first prize and a recording contract but, with all his talent and exposure, his albums never produced a hit—at least not yet. Go figure; Michael has a great look, a unique and soulful voice, and he plays guitar really well. Why he hasn't had a hit yet is beyond me.

When I think about it, it's really mind-blowing that I had hit records in four different decades. I'm not sure that will ever happen again and not because someone isn't good enough. I think it's harder to have a long career today than it's ever been. The world is changing so quickly now that the public forgets you almost before they get to know you. When people come to my concerts and tell me they've followed my career for fifty years I'm amazed, then humbled, and then extra-determined to give them a great show.

Will I ever retire? No. I absolutely love what I do—who wouldn't? First, I'd have to get a job, this isn't a job—it's every fifteen-year-old boy's dream! I mean, I go onstage and every three minutes the audience says, "You're wonderful!" And by the way, here's fifty thousand dollars for doing it.

I've come to the point where I feel my life has purpose. I think at least part of Bill Medley's purpose is to make people feel—and feel good. I'm not the kind of guy who can change the world, I'm not that bright. But if you come to see my show I can make you feel good. If I can make a phone call to a fan who's sick or dying and put a smile on their face, thank you, God.

If you want to know about me here's all you really need to know—I cry when I see a great commercial, I'm just that emotional. That's how I sing and that's how I feel. I love the underdog—I was an underdog and my heart goes out to those who struggle. I want people to remember me as someone who felt other people's emotions and understood.

Most of all, I hope you'll remember Bill Medley as a man who loved—that's righteous, brother.

Afterthoughts from the Coauthor

I had seen Bill Medley perform a few times and, like most, listened to his records hundreds of times. Years ago, at a special Valentine's Day show he was seated right next to me in the audience, I didn't even notice him. Then the bandleader called him up to sing "Lovin' Feelin'" and I sat there fascinated as he sang it to our table. I said to my date, "Do you know how cool this is?" Of course, at that time I had no idea I'd ever meet him, let alone work on his memoir.

When I went to his home to discuss the book idea I wasn't sure what to expect. I'd been a Vegas lounge performer when Bill and Bobby were tearing up the "big rooms" on the strip. I've met and worked with enough celebrities to know that many have a well-developed, sometimes over-developed sense of self. When I arrived I noticed an iron gate that guarded the walkway to his home and a buzzer to ask for permission to enter. I pressed the buzzer repeatedly, no answer. Finally I tried the gate and to my surprise it was unlocked. When I got to the front door I saw a sign that read "The Medleys"—whew, at least I was at the right house. There was a tattered piece of paper taped over the doorbell that looked like it had been there for years. It read, *Bell broken, please knock.*

I knocked. Again, no answer. "Man," I thought, "Do I have the right time, is he expecting me?" After several progressively louder knocks a distinguished older gentleman came to the door. He said, "Hey, have you been here long? My hearing isn't what it used to be. Bill's in the shower and he'll be down in a bit—I'm Nino." We sat and talked for a while and I figured out who he was; it was Nino Tempo, who'd made monster hit records in the 1960s with his sister April Stevens. He'd also been featured in one of my all-time favorite movies, *The Glenn Miller Story*, with Jimmy Stewart. Pretty cool.

OK, pleasant conversation—good start I thought. Next Bill's manager and close friend David Cohen arrived. If you needed a model for an old-time show-biz guy who'd been everywhere and seen everything, it would be David. He'd handled the business affairs of more stars than I could name. I was immediately taken by how real these guys were; clearly their days of needing to impress anyone had long passed.

After a bit Bill came downstairs. He couldn't have been more friendly or gracious, but it was obvious from the start that Bill, David, and Nino had no interest in fluff. It was like, "Why are we here, give us the headline." I showed them a recent book I'd written and some examples of others in the memoir vain, but Bill took the conversation in a whole other direction. He wanted to know about me—who I was. They told me they'd had multiple offers to write his memoir in the past but never found someone they thought could get it right.

I started talking about my life, my kids, and my past days in Vegas, and at one point I could see something clicked in Bill's head. He stopped the chit-chat and went into telling stories for the book. "Crap," I thought. I wasn't prepared to start working on it right then, but I took out a legal pad and began frantically writing down what he was saying. Bill is perhaps the best raconteur I've ever met. He tells stories like he sings, from the heart and with no qualms about opening his soul. I knew then we had something.

After another hour or so David took me into Bill's den and we discussed the terms of our arrangement. We agreed, shook hands and that was that. In subsequent weeks teams of lawyers wrote the contracts and they were exactly what David and I had agreed to with a simple handshake. His word and handshake was as good as anything ten lawyers could contrive—not many guys like that left in show business.

I found Bill to be the same; he says what he means and means what he says. I tell people I learned all I needed to know about who Bill Medley is on my first visit to his dressing room after a show. Many artists, especially those with his rich history, have extensive "riders" on their contracts regarding backstage food and facilities. I found Bill in a cramped dressing room making a bologna sandwich. He told me about his "food rider." Grocery store bologna, sliced onions, white bread, and plain yellow mustard. "None of that fancy deli stuff," he said. That was it. He told me, "You know, what I really love is a nice bologna sandwich after a show." He added, "Onions make everything taste better, don't they?"

That's Bill Medley. He knows what he likes and doesn't consider himself special. Class without pretension is how I would describe him. Sure, thanks to Paula, his home is decorated with exquisite taste—but Bill Medley is still a jeans and T-shirt guy. It seems everyone I interviewed for the book had the same take on Bill, a regular guy who knows how to be a friend. With Bill, if you're in, you're in. I came to discover that he doesn't let many in, but he's fiercely loyal to those he does.

Another thing that floored me about Bill is his commitment to excellence in performing. At this point, with all the hits and legacy, he could kind of "phone it in" and nobody would blame him. Recently in Vegas I watched him do his sound check before a show. He was meticulous, "Give me a little more guitar in my monitor, a little less reverb on McKenna's voice, etc." Not bossy or arrogant, just totally committed to getting it right. Then, after sound check he called some of the band members over and they did a vocal rehearsal on a song they'd probably done a hundred times. He wanted to change one of the harmony lines. Patiently he walked every member through, "Sing this line, go up a half step here, etc." I went up to him afterward and said, "Bill, you still really love what you do, don't you?"

With a slightly embarrassed grin he said, "Oh yeah." That night his sold-out audience loved it too. As for me—I always loved the music, now I love the man. Co-writing this book has been the time of my life.   *—Mike Marino*

Mike Marino is an author, speaker, and musician. He hosted a nationally syndicated call-in radio program for five years and has produced broadcast programming, live events, and written materials for such diverse people as Dr. Laura Schlessinger, PBS-TV's Daniel Amen, M.D., Reverend Billy Graham, and country music's LaDonna Gatlin. As a musician and performer, he made his first TV appearance at age five and was a member of several popular music groups—including the McCoys, famous for their #1 hit "Hang on Sloopy."

Acknowledgments

BILL MEDLEY

I want to thank all these wonderful people for their love, talent, friendship, and support. Barry Mann and Cynthia Weil, Jennifer Warnes, Paul Williams, Jimmy Webb, Lee Ferrell, Gary Stephens, Ronny May, Johnny Mohler, Judi Fields, Sandy Massman, Nino Tempo, Cook E. Jarr, Kenny Rogers, Keb Mo, Alabama, Jimmy Ienner, John Wimber, Mike Patterson, Barry Rillera, Darlene Love, Paul Revere, Steve and Velda Brooks, Jim and Cheryl West, Kathleen Maughan, Vivian Haworth, and Brad Garrett.

To all the great musicians who've honored me on the stage and in the studio, thanks for making the music sound so good. To my mom and dad, my brother Leon and his family, and my sister Barbara and her family—I love you all very much.

The truth is—I have friends, good friends, great friends, and soulmates. Three guys who moved into my soulmate category long ago are David Cohen, Jerry Perenchio, and Michael Gaughan. You guys mean the world to me.

I also want to thank Mike Marino for being such a great writer and turning into such a great friend, he did a phenomenal job with this book. Thanks also to Bobby Cruz for introducing us; it wouldn't have happened without you.

Of course, life wouldn't make sense without my wife, kids, and grandkids. To the most important person in my life, Paula, I love you with all my heart—yesterday, today, and forever. McKenna, Darrin, Damien, KC, Caylan, and Tyler—I love you more than you'll ever know and I'm so very proud of you all.

I'm sure I missed thanking some wonderful people who've helped shape my life. To anyone I missed—if you're not in the book, please know you're in my heart.

MIKE MARINO

I want to thank Bill; working with him was every writer's dream. He's a great storyteller and his unvarnished vulnerability made this project a joy. Thanks also to my wonderful friend Bobby Cruz, who introduced us. He told me, "With Bill, what you see is what you get." Bobby was spot-on.

In typical Medley fashion, Paula, Darrin, and McKenna also opened their arms and hearts to help and I am deeply grateful. Everyone I interviewed for the book graciously surrendered their time and memories, and seeing Bill through their eyes painted the picture with fascinating color and texture—thanks to all.

Thanks to my agent, Michael Harriot, for your steadfast and patient efforts to see this book come to reality, and also to our editor Ben Schafer, your enthusiasm for this book was super encouraging.

To the men of my Saturday morning group, who've stood with me through the good and bad for over 10 years, thanks for being genuine friends. To my best friend, my father Joe Marino, you inspire me every single day. To my beautiful kids—Mallory, Joey, and Marisa, you've given my life meaning and purpose beyond what I could have hoped for; it's an honor to be your dad.

Index